ANGOLAN WAR OF LIBERATION

COLONIAL–COMMUNIST CLASH
1961–1974

AL J. VENTER

Pen & Sword
MILITARY

First published in Great Britain in 2018 by
PEN AND SWORD MILITARY
an imprint of
Pen and Sword Books Ltd
47 Church Street
Barnsley
South Yorkshire S70 2AS

Copyright © Al J. Venter, 2018

Typeset by Aura Technology and Software Services, India
Printed and bound in Malta by Gutenberg

ISBN 978 1 526728 41 8

Pen & Sword Books Ltd incorporates the imprints of Pen & Sword
Archaeology, Atlas, Aviation, Battleground, Discovery, Family History, History, Maritime, Military,
Naval, Politics, Railways, Select, Social History, Transport, True Crime, Claymore Press, Frontline
Books, Leo Cooper, Praetorian Press, Remember When, Seaforth Publishing and Wharncliffe.

For a complete list of Pen and Sword titles please contact
Pen and Sword Books Limited
47 Church Street, Barnsley, South Yorkshire, S70 2AS, England
email: enquiries@pen-and-sword.co.uk
website: www.pen-and-sword.co.uk

CONTENTS

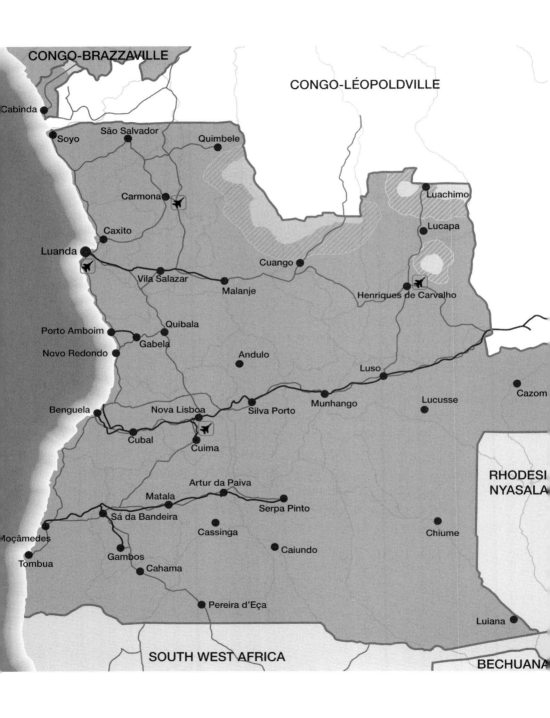

GLOSSARY

AAA	anti-aircraft artillery
AK/ AK-47	*Avtomat Kalashnikova* 7.62mm assault rifle
aldeamento	protected village
APC	armoured personnel carrier
assimilado	Africans overseas who had 'assimilated' sufficiently to earn full Portuguese citizenship rights
BMP-2	*Boyevaya Mashina Pekhoty*, Soviet amphibious tracked infantry fighting vehicle
BRDM	*Boyevaya Razvedyvatelnaya Dozomaya Mashina*, 4x4 (converting to 8x8) amphibious combat reconnaissance patrol vehicle
BTR	*Bronetransportyor*, armoured transporter, 8x8 armoured personnel carrier
CAS sorties	close air support sorties
chefe do poste	local Portuguese administrator
CIA	Central Intelligence Agency (US)
COIN	counterinsurgency
DGS	(Portuguese) *Direcçao General de Segurança*, General Security Directorate
DShK	*Degtyaryova-Shpagina Krupnokaliberny*, Soviet 12.7mm heavy antiaircraft machine gun
FAL	*Fusil Automatique Léger* (light automatic rifle), a self-loading, selective-fire battle rifle produced by the Belgian armaments manufacturer Fabrique Nationale de Herstal (FN).
FALA	UNITA's military wing
FAP	*Força Aerea Portuguesa*, Portuguese Air Force *also* PAF
FLEC	Front for the Liberation of Cabinda
FNLA	*Frente Nacional de Libertação de Angola*, National Front for the Liberation of Angola
G3	7.62mm battle rifle developed in the 1950s by the German armament manufacturer Heckler & Koch GmbH (H&K) in collaboration with the Spanish. Adapted by the Portuguese armed forces
GPMG	general-purpose machine gun

GRAE	*Govêrno Revolucionário de Angola no Exílo,* Revolutionary Government of Angola in Exile
Grupos Especiais	Portuguese Army Special Force units
Grupos Especiais Pára-Quedistas	Paratrooper Special Groups (volunteer black soldiers with parachute training)
IFV	infantry fighting vehicle
Katyusha	Soviet 122mm multiple rocket launcher
KGB	*Komitet gosudarstevennoy bezopasnosti,* (Soviet) Committee for State Security.
KIA	killed in action
LZ	landing zone
MAG	*Mitrailleuse d'Appui Général,* Belgian FN 7.62mm general-purpose machine gun
MANPAD	man-portable air defence system (like the Soviet Strela)
metrópole-províncias ultramarinas	Portuguese overseas provinces
MG 42	*Maschinengewehr* 42, a general-purpose machine gun, originally German and much favoured by Portuguese ground troops in all three African theatres of war
MPLA	*Movimento Popular de Libertàcao de Angola,* Popular Movement for the Liberation of Angola
OAU	Organization of African Unity, today African Union
PAF	Portuguese Air Force *also* FAP
Panhard AML	*Automitrailleuse légère,* light 4x4 armoured car, developed by South Africa into the Eland
Panhard EBR	*Engin Blindé de Reconnaissance,* French-built, light 8x8 armoured vehicle
PCA	Angolan Communist Party
PIDE	*Polícia Internacional e de Defesa do Estado,* International Police for the Defence of the State (Lisbon's equivalent of the secret police)
POM-Z	Soviet anti-personnel stake-mounted fragmentation mine, much used in Africa
RPD	Soviet-made 7.62mm light machine gun
RPG	rocket propelled grenade, either RPG-2 (used by guerrillas in Portuguese African conflicts), or latterly, RPG-7 with additional variations
RPK	Soviet-made 7.62mm light machine gun

SAAF	South African Air Force
SAM	surface-to-air missile, SA-6, SA-8 et al
SAP	South African Police
SNEB	*Societe Nouvelle des Etablissements Edgar Brandt* 37mm Matra unguided air-to-ground rocket
T-34 and T-55/ T-54	Soviet tanks supplied to Angola and Mozambique
TM-46 and TM-57	Soviet anti-tank mines used by liberation groups
Tropas Especiais	Special Troops, commonly known by the acronym TEs, which came into effect when a UPA/ FNLA guerrilla defected to the Portuguese with 1,200 of his men
UNITA	*União Nacional Para a Independência Total de Angola*, National Union for the Total Liberation of Angola
UPA	*União dos Populacèes de Angola,* Patriotic Union of Angola

INTRODUCTION

In 1961, Portugal found itself fighting a war to retain its colonial possessions in a desperate bid to preserve the historical remnants of its Empire. Under its dictator Antonio de Salazar, an economist by profession who had taken over the country in 1932 and was already seventy years old when the African wars started, both he and his nation were almost completely unprepared to do what was needed to repel an invasion of large numbers of hostile revolutionaries from the Congo.

Lisbon knew it was coming, or rather that hostile forces would stoke a revolt, but nobody was prepared for the sheer scale of thousands of half-clad primitives swarming into Angola to overthrow the government.

The army and the navy were guarding the colony and they would soon start cracking heads and turning the recalcitrants on their heels, Lisbon responded, adding that any kind of uprising by the locals would be suicide. The consensus in Europe was that it had happened before and always failed: in the upper echelons of state it was believed that this revolt would also collapse.

Portugal poured troops into the colony as fast as its creaking logistic system would allow, but at the start, most of those efforts were piecemeal. The guerrillas made a lot of headway, grabbed several northern towns and even managed to establish a revolutionary government in a small colonial settlement in Angola's northern jungles. They called it The Socialist Republic of Nambuangongo.

In April 1961, when the assault came, Portugal sought to deploy its forces as rapidly as possible to the territory to restore order. While some troops such as the paratroopers were airlifted to Africa, the majority came from the *metrópole*, or continental Portugal, by ocean transport, a lengthy and expensive business. Between the months of May and December 1961, troop strength was augmented from about 8,000 security personnel, army and police to something like 35,000.

The troops landed in Luanda and, as they became available over this eight-month period, the majority were deployed in bids to subdue the escalating threat and regain control in the north of the colonial territory. This transition from a small colonial force aimed at reaction, defence and subjective rule to a large one of reoccupation and neutralization was gradual: it was dependent both on transportation resources that were not designed for military power projection and the reorientation of ground and air forces to counter a modern guerrilla insurrection, something that almost none had faced before.

To be fair, the guerrillas had similar problems, probably worse because many had been hauled off the streets in the villages and towns where they lived, the fortunate

Angola was a tough war, fought by resolute adversaries in extremely difficult conditions—an army convoy struggles in northern Angola.

ones given a rifle and ordered to head into the jungle and get on with it. The uprising teetered along, the rebels neither adequately armed nor trained and for the most part illiterate and brutal.

Squads of new Portuguese army arrivals—equally new to the game—were pushed northward from Luanda and soon displayed their own inadequacies. Indeed, government forces were not competent; those involved were badly trained and ill-equipped and did not possess the skills needed to fight what had transmogrified into a vicious counterinsurgency. As one observer pointed out at the time, while any form of military retaliation, by its nature, requires substantial numbers of light infantry, the force sent in to do the necessary must first be trained in the craft of fighting a 'small war' to be effective; second, it has to display a measure of determination, if only to get the job done.

In Lisbon's new emergency, that was not the case because in those early days Portugal did not have the ability to alter age-old traditions. The last time its army had fought a significant battle was during World War I when German forces invaded both Angola and Mozambique and had given Lisbon's troops a thorough drubbing. In truth, the majority of Portugal's forces arriving in Angola in 1961 had no real military orientation and matters were compounded because these troops had to be made ready to fight at an accelerated pace. Even their uniforms were hastily crafted and not ideally suited to fighting in the African bush. Their weapons, too, were dismal. When the war started, the Portuguese were still using antiquated Karabiner 98k rifles—a controlled-feed bolt-action rifle based on the venerated Mauser M 98 system

Above left: Army battalion insignia, the entrance to a base.

Above right: President Antonio de Salazar who took his nation to war.

that traced its roots to the Lebel Model 1886—with some units equipped with the pre-World War I German MG 13.[*]

And while some rebels had Kalashnikovs, the majority of the invading force did not. In fact, some of them were armed with their trusty old 19th-century flintlocks that they had used for generations to hunt. The vast majority had machetes and spears, but when a defending force of a few dozen is faced with a surge of a thousand or more screaming belligerents headed in their direction, only a fool would stand and fight.

In reoccupying the north and addressing the enemy threat, Portugal quickly realized that its most effective forces were those with special qualifications and advanced training: unfortunately there were only small numbers of such elite forces. The maturing experiences of the Portuguese in those early days during which anything could happen—and the tactical advantage swung to and fro—the consequential

---

[*] The Karabiner was actually a fine weapon. I used one with open sights to hunt an eland for one unit's supply of meat while embedded in one of the Portuguese Army camps in the southeast of the country and, as expected, it delivered a single-shot kill. But it could hardly compare with a fully automatic AK-47.

Gathering of guerrillas prior to an attack. (Nordic Africa Institute)

adjustments of the colonial Portuguese to fight a counterinsurgency war had to lead to the creation of many more specialized units to narrow the gap between the ability of the insurgents to take the initiative and government forces to respond.

That initiative started to emerge among the defenders very early on, in large part because the rebels—now referring to themselves as 'liberating' guerrillas—were not at all organized, and unquestionably, liquor and drugs had a lot to do with it. Both the MPLA and UPA/ FNLA certainly shared very little with the ability, for instance, of the Viet Cong or Algeria's FLN to effectively fight a war. There were two dissident political groupings in the Congolese capital Leopoldville at the time, the *Movimento Popular de Libertação de Angola* or People's Movement for the Liberation of Angola (MPLA) which displayed a clear Marxist, anti-colonial penchant and the *União das Populações de Angola* (UPA), which became the National Front for the Liberation of Angola (FNLA) a year after the revolution started.

For the Marxist 'Popular Movement' this soon changed. A group of Moscow hardliners started to take control and dictated the way things should be run and what would happen to those who were not prepared to accept the dictates of the so-called 'New Order'. The MPLA's Agostinho Neto was true to his word when he declared that he would "bring the revolution to the people of Angola" and any-body—man or woman—who stood in his way was to be quietly taken into the jungle and shot.

Away from the main road, such as that was, it was always difficult country, in Cabinda especially.

Essentially, Angola's war might never have happened had the colonizers not been so severe on their subjects. Work conditions for the average labourer in the colonies—and this applied to Angola as well as Mozambique, Portuguese Guinea and the off-shore islands of São Tomé and Cape Verde—were atrocious. Pay was minimal and any money earned usually had to be spent in company stores owned by the employers, most times with prices inflated. So the capitalists gained both ways: from their workers and fairly good returns from the money paid to that labour in buying goods from company shops. If anybody complained or resisted this kind of exploitation, they were brutally dealt with by the police. Deaths of suspects in custody were not uncommon.

Events leading up to what is today referred as the 'Baixa de Cassanje Revolt' started with a boycott by workers who had been labouring in extensive cottonfields owned by the Cotonang Company which belonged to a European cartel of Portuguese, British and German investors. The boycott was led by two aspiring young political firebrands Antonio Mariano and Kulu-Xingu who urged workers to burn their identification cards and then encouraged them to attack Portuguese traders. This revolt caused a lot of damage and injuries but, as far as is known, no deaths, though the authorities in Luanda, the Angolan capital, claimed otherwise. The local governor of the territory sent in the air force in reply and bombed twenty villages. Critics of this action claimed the Portuguese used bombs and napalm and that there were more than 400 deaths, but the truth is another story.*

Unquestionably, there was a lot of damage done in these retaliatory raids and after that, many of the local population retreated into the bush. The large groups of rebels that had entered the country had very clearly been prepared for just such an eventuality. The bottom line here is that it was all planned beforehand and there is a lot of evidence: groups of rebels gathered just across the unmarked Congolese frontier, some having been trained in other countries, as well as the clear distribution of weapons and ammunition. Though limited, this did make a difference in the ultimate objective of trying to drive the settlers off their lands and from their shops and factories and finally, a command structure, though primal and lacking communications, became almost fit for purpose.

Initially military activities were restricted to the regions immediately north of Luanda, at one stage penetrating to within about forty kilometres of the capital before the guerrillas were driven back. But already there were a perspicacious few in the Portuguese capital who acknowledged that conditions had deteriorated to the point where Angola was faced with the prospect of a full-scale civil war. More to the point, they were not afraid to say to so to their superiors.

For once, the unusually reticent President Salazar listened and he had good reason to do so because this is what happened:

Earlier, on 4 February 1961, using arms which had been captured from Portuguese soldiers and police, MPLA guerrillas attacked Luanda's São Paulo fortress prison and police headquarters in Luanda in an attempt to free a bunch of political prisoners who were being held there. While the attack was unsuccessful and no prisoners were released, seven Portuguese policemen and forty Angolans were killed, mostly MPLA insurgents. The authorities responded with alacrity in a series of sweeping counterinsurgency responses in which over 5,000 Angolans were arrested. Thereafter, a Luanda mob, almost all of them white, raided the city's shanty towns—*musseques*—and killed dozens in the process.

In a draft thesis written by two Stanford University students, James Fearon and David Laitin, in 2005, titled 'Portugal' the sequence of events is very well encapsulated. Several factors helped translate these grievances into actual revolution, say Fearon

---

* There were many overblown casualty figures, principally the 10,000 'native dead' offered by the UPA after it initially asserted 7,000. Others include 5,000 by José Ervedosa, an extreme left-winger who eventually decamped to revolutionary Algeria. Also, the issue of "hundreds, perhaps thousands dead" by the French historian René Pélissier, who vividly describes mass graves dug by bulldozers, of which there was none operating in Baixa do Cassange in the rainy season. Also, the dates given for the use of napalm bombs conflicted with heavy tropical downpours when all flights were suspended. Napalm was used in the war but not then, which raises the issue about other claims made.

Above left: One of the answers to the war was to gather locals in protected villages or *aldeamentos*, one seen here over the barrel of a 20mm cannon.

Above right: A Panhard AML-60 armoured car.

and Laitin. First, quite a few neighbouring African countries were in the process of either getting their independence or planning for the official handover of power. This included the two Congos, one formerly Belgian and the other, Congo-Brazzaville, which had been administered under the Tricolor for half a century or more.[*]

On Angola's eastern limits, Northern Rhodesia was soon to become Zambia and still farther east, Tanganyika was about to embrace *Uhuru* (kiSwahili for Freedom) under the guidance of a radical graduate of Edinburgh University by the name of Julius Nyerere who made no secret of his socialist predilections.

Algeria's *Front de Libération Nationale* (FLN)—still struggling in its own war of independence from France—supplied the UPA movement (then headquartered in Leopoldville) with modern weapons, while Tunisia and Congo provided training camps. The newly created Organization of African Unity recognized the proto-insurgent group as Angola's government-in-exile in 1963.

---

[*] There are two Congos that share the river by that name in Central Africa. The one was originally a French colony with its capital at Brazzaville—that is Congo (Brazza), or more formally the Republic of the Congo. The other Congo is the Democratic Republic of the Congo, formerly a Belgian possession also referred to in its day as Congo (Kinshasa) but no longer.

With Zambia's independence in 1964, the MPLA was able to open an eastern front two years later, but it was always tough going for the guerrillas operating from there. It was a long way from the Zambian frontier to the population centres of Luanda, added to which enemy columns were isolated and vulnerable to attack. Also, there were few locals who had either food or intelligence to share and rebel columns had to cross a colossal vastness and in the process would invariably leave a trail that in the soft sand of the region could be easily tracked. While the guerrillas kept trying, it ended up being largely self-defeating. So it was no surprise when finally, in 1973, the MPLA gave up trying in the East and Jonas Savimbi's UNITA (*União Nacional para a Independência Total de Angola*) guerrillas quickly filled the gap, much of which was their own Ovimbundu tribal homeland. Related to this, the Afro-Asian and communist bloc—at the time vigorously pushing for decolonization in the UN—gave aid to the rebels through the auspices of the recently formed Non-Aligned Movement.

Second, in 1961—to the shock of Salazar—President Kennedy voted against Portugal in the Security Council on a recommendation concerning Portugal's reprisals against Angolan insurgencies. The move might have been partially motivated by the CIA placing Holden Roberto, the leader of the UPA/ FNLA on its payroll, probably in an effort to keep the Chinese and Russians at arms' length. It helped that President Mobuto of Congo/ Zaire was Roberto's brother-in-law.

Third, the Portuguese reluctantly allowed Protestant missionaries to work in the colonies and it says a lot that the three leading insurgents in Angola were all educated by these missionaries: Roberto by the Baptists, Neto by Methodists and Savimbi by the Congregationalists.

Meanwhile, many Angolans who had served as soldiers in the Portuguese army or security forces deserted and crossed into the Congo where Roberto was forming his ELNA (*Exército de Libertação Nacional de Angola*), the forerunner to the FNLA, with camps in the Congo and a military counsel from the Algerian liberation movement. Within six months the war was in full swing.

From today's perspective, it seems barely credible that between the years 1961 and 1974 Portugal fought three separate wars in Angola, Mozambique and Guinea-Bissau. Those African countries were colonial possessions of Portugal and taken together, were more than twenty times the size of the *metrópole*, as the 'motherland' was referred to by its African subjects. At the time, Portugal was an impoverished country—the second poorest in Europe, presumably after Albania—with a population of just nine million and a small and underfunded military, even though it was a member of NATO. Yet Lisbon managed to run several military campaigns in Africa for longer than the US army was officially deployed in Vietnam. Also, it did so with an astonishing doggedness and degree of effectiveness for much of that time, irrespective of some almost crippling logistical challenges.

By 1974 the military campaigns were consuming nearly half of Portugal's GDP and to outside observers—and quite a few in Portugal itself—it appeared to be a clearly unsustainable effort. But things staggered along like this for thirteen years and it was only in April 1974 when a coup in Lisbon resulted in a change of government and a rapid end to Portugal's empire. In the broader context, the Portuguese armed forces could never have hoped to win, but then nor were they defeated in the conventional sense.

In fact, only when the so-called 'Carnation Revolution' of 1974 came to pass did most Americans realize that Portugal had been fighting three 'Vietnams' at one time and, in a few respects, with somewhat better success than the United States had achieved in South East Asia.

The 'carnation' appellation refers to Portuguese soldiers putting flowers into the barrels of their rifles to indicate support for the army mutiny in Lisbon. It might be apocryphal, but it is said that an old woman threw a bunch of red carnations at some soldiers as they passed her house and one of them lodged in the barrel of his rifle.

What is also difficult to grasp is that Portugal still had several African colonies up to the mid-1970s, when pretty much the entire colonial bandwagon had been left behind a decade or more before. And what went on in Angola, Mozambique and Portuguese Guinea (today Guiné-Bissau) was also on a very different scale than Vietnam. Helicopter assaults and bombings, while not rare, were not nearly as commonplace as was the case in South East Asia, as were fully direct confrontations between the

Marines take the initiative in Angola. (Revista de Militar)

insurgents and government forces. The norm, as I was to observe for myself during several operational visits in all three dependencies, was more of the nature of cat-and-mouse skirmishes: slow, constant attrition, point and counter-point, as it were. Above all, the struggles could be likened to a series of conflicting 'wars of wills'.

Portuguese pride had a lot to do with it, the need for Lisbon to maintain the all-embracing self-image of a colonizing powerhouse, and sadly, it kept the country stuck in a war it couldn't win for almost a decade and a half. As someone commented after it was all over, there was obviously a crucial imbalance of determination between the colonies and Portugal.

Commonly referred to as Lisbon's overseas war or, in the colonies, the wars of liberation, these struggles played a seminal role in ending white rule in southern Africa. After the Lisbon army mutiny of 1974, it took just another five years for the Rhodesian bush war to play itself out and the country's white settlers, at Britain's behest, to hand over power to Robert Mugabe.

Portugal's guerrilla wars in Africa were fought under horrendous conditions, made worse by a continent that has never been kind to the interloper. Interestingly, things weren't nearly as bad in Angola, where generations of young Portuguese had lived and worked in this remote and remarkably wealthy bush country. Primitive it might have been, but Angola's natural resources included diamonds, gold and oil and offered undreamed-of rewards to those who persevered. The country's farming community in the pre-revolutionary days was among the most successful in Africa and Angolan coffee was legendary. More to the point, the always-hardy Portuguese appeared to adapt easily to adversity. Those who had been there for generations often enough understood conditions better than their black compadres, which was a reason why the war in Angola ultimately went a lot better than it did in Mozambique.

The majority of young conscripts, from their homes in Oporto, Sintra, Coimbra, Figuera de Fos and elsewhere, often faced a host of uncompromising options. Like many American GIs in Asia, the majority were still in their teens, thrust into a series of bitter conflicts that ultimately went on to claim some 10,000 Portuguese lives.

Stuck in the African bush, sometimes for years at stretch, coupled to austere, harsh living conditions, as well as the prospect of contracting any one of dozens of tropical illnesses, their options were limited. Malaria, tick bite fever and other insect-borne diseases were always a factor and though Lisbon seemed to cope, these remote regions exacted a steady toll. No wonder then that tens of thousands of young men of military age from the western fringe of the Iberian Peninsula voted with their feet. Most slipped quietly across the border into Spain and made their way to Germany, France, Scandinavia and elsewhere to find jobs and sit out the war. Yet, by the time it all ended, we are told by the noted American historian, former naval aviator Dr John P. 'Jack' Cann, Lisbon had ruled its African territories for almost five centuries, not always undisputed by its black and *mestizo* subjects, but effectively enough to create a lasting Lusitanian tradition. That imprint is indelible and remains engraved in language, social mores and cultural traditions that sometimes have more in common with Europe than with Africa. Most of the Portuguese soldiers who fought these African struggles were young and impoverished, and in some cases, undernourished. Though there was great enthusiasm among the defenders to start with, these youngsters—the majority straight from school on two- and three-year tours of duty—felt they were being dragged into a meaningless conflict. One of the consequences was that they did the minimum until their campaign was over.

At the same time, it was sad to see, as in any conflict, how the local population suffered the most severe blows. They were pushed hard and often brutally both by government forces and revolutionaries.

It is also important to look back and observe how the guerrillas were manipulated by a host of alien backgrounds. Apart from Algeria, Tanzania and the others, many insurgents were trained in China where they were taught to incorporate the trusted tactics implemented by Mao Zedong in his own civil war as well as those of Che Guevara, into a strictly African context, like using primeval bush to their advantage, propaganda, limited mobility and living off the land. It was the start of a Cold War 'mission creep' into an almost moribund colonialism.

As one American commentator declared, "to counter this, Lisbon did a terrific job of trying to effectively wage, and win essentially three Vietnam-styled wars all at the same time."

Lisbon's forces had no end of transport problems in Angola.

Some Portuguese units fared better than most. Dr Cann has written several books that deal with some of Lisbon's elite fighting units. He declares in the introduction to his own volume on the role of the Portuguese commandos in Africa, or as they were referred to locally *comandos Africanos** that during the thirteen-year insurgency, roughly 800,000 men and a small number of women, mostly in medical and communications roles, served in the Portuguese armed forces.

Of this number, about 9,000 served in the field as commandos (about one percent). Yet their combat losses—357 dead, 28 missing in action and 771 wounded—represented 11.5 percent of the total casualties (a percentage ten times that of normal troops).

It is well established that these warriors were responsible for the elimination of more insurgents and the capture of more of their weapons than any other combat unit during the war. Great pains were taken to stay abreast of the latest enemy operational methods and maintain the 'warrior edge.' This edge, basically, was an approach to fighting that pushed the commandos always to think of themselves as the hunter rather than the hunted.

Officers returning from contact with the enemy were rigorously debriefed, and commando instructors regularly participated in operations to learn of the latest enemy developments. Information gained was integrated with intelligence from other sources gathered by the military and national intelligence services, and from this current knowledge, training was constantly revised to remain attuned to the enemy and his behaviour.

The commandos became a breed apart—and their reputation was such that when insurgents discovered a Special Forces unit deployed into their area, they would generally withdraw until the 'killers' had left.

The same with the Portuguese Air Force and here Cann is even more explicit: following the 1952 reorganization of the Portuguese Air Force from the army and naval air arms, Lisbon now had an entity dedicated solely to aviation that would bring it into line with its new NATO commitment. As it proceeded to develop a competence in modern multi-engine and jet fighter aircraft for its NATO role and train a professional corps of pilots, it was suddenly confronted in 1961 with fighting several insurgencies in Africa. This development forced it to acquire an entirely new and separate air force, the so-called African Air Force, to address this emerging danger.

Aircraft available at the time were largely castoffs from the larger, richer, and more sophisticated air forces of its NATO partners and not specifically designed for

---

* John P. Cann, *Portuguese Commandos: Feared Insurgent Hunters, 1961–1974.*

General Bettencourt Rodrigues (right) turned the war in Angola around.

counterinsurgency. Yet Portugal adapted them to the task at hand and effectively crafted the appropriate strategies and tactics for their successful deployment.

"Advances in weaponry, such as the helicopter gunship, were the outgrowth of combat needs. The acquired logistic competences assured that the needed fuel types and lubricants, spare parts, and qualified maintenance personnel were available in even the most remote African backwaters.

"So too with advanced flying skills such as visual reconnaissance and air–ground coordinated fire support: all were honed and perfected. All of these aspects and more are explored and hold lessons in the application of airpower in any insurgency today," declared Cann in what is unquestionably one of the best books to emerge from those African campaigns.[*] It is interesting that Portuguese marines, the *Fuzileiros*, underwent one of the longest and most physically demanding specialist infantry training regimes in the world, lasting some forty-two weeks. Perhaps only fifteen to thirty five percent of the inductees eventually passed the course and were awarded the traditional and highly coveted navy blue beret, says Cann.

---

[*] John P Cann, *Flight Plan Africa*: *Portuguese Airpower in Counterinsurgency, 1961–1974*.

1. UNFOLDING

4 February 1961

A small group of Africans, all linked to the political group *Movimento Popular de Libertação de Angola* (MPLA) attacked Luanda Prison. This political grouping was originally established in the pre-1960s when the tiny underground Angolan Communist Party (PCA) linked up with liked-minded dissidents.

The Portuguese initially had 8,000 men in Angola when the 1961 attacks occurred: roughly 3,000 Portuguese military and security personnel (including police) and 5,000 Africans, but this figure is deceptive as this tiny combined force had to control events in a country a dozen times larger than the size of Portugal.

Lisbon's colonial war (*Guerra Colonial Portuguesa*), also known in Portugal as the Overseas War (*Guerra do Ultramar*) and among the guerrillas as the War of Liberation (*Guerra de Libertação*) was a long, drawn-out and extremely bitter campaign from the start, but the insurgents, having battled almost to the gates of Luanda lost their initial momentum and were gradually pushed back into the jungle.

MPLA guerrilla leader Agostinho Neto reviews his troops.

What was surprising about this jungle war was that there were not many more ambushes.

The Portuguese initially reacted to the uprising with great violence. Many of their own people had been slaughtered—roughly 400 settlers within the first few weeks of the uprising. Local Portuguese communities quickly organized themselves into vigilante committees, and for several months after the violence started, reprisals went uncontrolled by civilian and military authorities. Whites' treatment of Africans was every bit as brutal and arbitrary as that of the rebels toward them. Fear pervaded the country for a long time, driving an even deeper wedge between the races. The number of Africans who died as a result of the 1961 uprisings has been estimated as high as 40,000, many of whom succumbed from disease or famine. Apart from Europeans killed, hundreds of *assimilados* and Africans deemed sympathetic to colonial authorities were also slaughtered.

By the summer of 1961 the Portuguese had reduced the area controlled by the rebels to about a half its original extent, but major pockets of resistance remained. Portuguese forces, relying heavily on air power, attacked villages. The result was the mass exodus of Africans toward the Congo.

From then on, with Lisbon pushing its air force and more troops into the hostilities, the struggle became one of grinding attrition and went on for thirteen years. The end of the war came suddenly with an army mutiny—the Carnation Revolution—launched by dissident young officers in Lisbon in April 1974.

18 March 1967

There were thousands of incidents that characterized the nature of the guerrilla struggle that started when a large group of insurgents crossed the border from the Congo, itself in a state of revolt with little and—in some areas—no effective government. The invasion was not coordinated and had no fixed objective apart from killing Portuguese farmers, administrators, traders and residents in a string of small towns scattered about a region half the size of Britain. Government troops arrived soon afterward, but their efforts were fruitless: a handful facing a much bigger rebel force. From there, hostilities escalated as thousands more revolutionaries entered northern Angola and rampaged, seemingly with nothing to stop them striking hard, as far south as Luanda, the capital.

The Dembos, northern Angola: 1967

The Dembos was the focus of much of the insurgent activity in northern Angola in the early days of the war. This heavily foliated, and largely mountainous jungle region starts roughly seventy kilometres north of Luanda. The terrain is rugged, broken sporadically by grey-blue granite peaks and, apart from isolated farmland and local towns and villages, most of it totally undeveloped. The insurgents used the peaks as observation points. The only way into the region during the earlier phases was a single road leading north out of Luanda, but this was poorly maintained and unsurfaced. As a consequence, military road convoys—to which civilian trucks would be attached—had a difficult time because the insurgents were active. It could take a day or more to cover a hundred kilometres by vehicle, twice that in the rainy season. An outward convoy might be attacked four or five times; the return trip was worse because the insurgents would be more prepared, having observed the trucks coming through on the outward leg. Soviet landmines were laid on all roads and tracks to disrupt traffic from the early days of the revolution.

Sector A

Setting: northern Angola lay just north of Sector/ Comsec D (and the Dembos mountains). This region stretched all the way to the Congo border and the coast to the west of Matadi, the main Congolese port on the great river. It was a wild, primitive and difficult area, much of it jungle swampland. Malaria and other tropical illnesses were rife. The sector was virtually uninhabited and the few Africans that remained tended to avoid both the Portuguese and insurgents because they simply did not want to get involved in the killings.

To reach Sector D the insurgents travelled either from Congo-Brazzaville or Leopoldville (later Kinshasa) and had to traverse Sector A, which lay flush with the frontier. It took the average insurgent six weeks to cover the 200-kilometre trail. They carried everything needed for the war on their backs—guns, ammunition, explosives, food, medical supplies, landmines and propaganda leaflets—which also suggests that the invasion was not as spontaneous as government opponents would have liked to believe. Eventually they were hauling in 250kg aerial bombs on litters, carried between four or more men (not that these made good for mine-laying as the security forces spotted them easily).

Sector D

Setting: Comsec D, Dembos mountains lay at the heart of the Portuguese counterinsurgency campaign in northern Angola. The sector was about the size of Cyprus and Santa Eulalia camp was its headquarters. There were seven other Portuguese camps in the sector, including Zala to the north of the sector, Zemba in the south and Nambuangongo ('Nambu') toward the centre, as well as Quicabo camp.

Sector F

Sector F adjoined Sector D and the Dembos. Terreiro was a small coffee-producing area in Sector F, just north of Santa Eulalia.

Santa Eulalia camp

The headquarters of Comsec D was constructed soon after the 1961 attacks. The camp straddled a group of low-lying hills and was built within what had once been a successful coffee estate. Around the camp was a patchwork of thousands of rows of coffee bushes, offset by open grassland along the perimeter, and beyond the plantation, the jungle. Garrisoned by 300 men, the commander at the time of the author's visit in 1969 was Brigadier Martins Soares. He had six staff officers to help cope with the counterinsurgency.

The layout of Santa Eulalia was typical of most Portuguese camps in Angola. The perimeter was a two-metre, barbed-wire double fence. Arc lights with protective wire coverings were spaced every three or four metres, but at night their lights could only penetrate fifty or so metres beyond the fence line because of foliage overhang. There were half a dozen machine-gun turrets spread about along the camp

Airdrop onto a remote camp in the Dembos.

24

perimeter. The central part of the camp had a row of low prefabricated wooden bungalows. An elaborate (by African standards) bunker and tunnel system supplemented these defences. The tunnels meant it was possible to move between the buildings and some of the forward positions in relative safety.

Unlike most other jungle camps in the region, Santa Eulalia had a second section near the airstrip for air force personnel. The army provided security for this as well as its own emplacements.

The garrison was highly mobile and provided tactical support for other Portuguese army units in the area. Their mobility came from the two dozen trucks—mostly West German-built Unimogs—as well as helicopters that routinely touched down at the base. Portuguese Air Force Alouette III helicopters all operated from a central base adjacent to Luanda's main international airport and rarely overnighted in the interior except in emergencies.

Nambuangongo ('Nambu') camp

Nambuangongo ('Nambu') camp was situated on a modest mountain in Sector D. It had been the officially declared insurgent headquarters in 1961 and fighting in the area had been fierce and consistent from the start. Portuguese army and police losses in the area were relatively high. Retaking Nambuangongo by government troops had been a "significant moral and military victory" for the government, so the insurgents constantly attacked the camp.

'Ambush Alley' on the way to the Dembos.

Quicabo camp

Quicabo was a Portuguese camp in the Dembos mountains of northern Angola with a garrison of 200 men. Because of the difficulty of road transport Quicabo got most of its supplies by air. Portuguese Air Force Nord Noratlas supply planes normally dropped their loads from around two hundred metres, with the final approach just above tree level. Once over the camp the transporters would make several passes and make their drops, usually two pallets at a time. The first had the mail, considered the most important cargo. Other supplies were fresh provisions for two or three days plus medical supplies. The terrain was difficult but occasionally the insurgents would attempt to target the aircraft on approach.

Zemba camp

Zemba army camp lay about twenty kilometres southeast of Santa Eulalia. It was overlooked by a large bald sugarloaf mountain to its south: the insurgents sometimes used it or the surrounding bush to fire into the camp or at aircraft, and, indeed, the camp came under attack just about every week since the start of operations. The garrison was composed mostly of infantry and patrolled the area either on foot or in trucks for which it had about a dozen Unimogs. The men followed a set patrol

Fuzileiros (marines) patrol in Congo mangrove swamps.

rota: so many days out (until dark) followed by a day or two of rest. The insurgents referred to the Portuguese patrols as 'death walkers' because the casualty rate was above average compared to other bases in the region. Lying south of the Dembos, there was more grassland than jungle, which, I was told by the commander, made insurgent ambushes less likely.

Portuguese-aligned civilians and local security in Sector D

By 1969 the local Africans of the Dembos generally worked their fields or settler plantations during the day and moved closer to the Portuguese camps for protection at night. The men were armed and organized into platoons under a section leader who reported to a Portuguese officer.

Even with the war, Sector D nurtured fairly large coffee estates, but because free movement could sometimes be dangerous, farmers struggled to hold back the jungle and some plantations were gradually overgrown. No soldiers were stationed in the fields. All farm owners and workers, white and black, were, within reason, responsible for their own security and all were armed with automatic weapons provided by the military. Farmers could fight off small insurgent attacks without help and were in radio contact with the nearest camp if it was felt that more firepower was needed.

Insurgents in Sector D

In 1969 the Portuguese estimated there were an estimated 5,000 to 6,000 insurgents in Sector D. Almost all had walked into Angola from the two Congos. By the time the author arrived, they were fighting in small units of about twenty men or less. Most had been trained outside Angola—in Zambia, Congo-Brazzaville, Algeria, Egypt, Tanzania or farther afield. Some had AK-47s and Simonov (SKS) carbines but others used a homemade blunderbuss that fired nails or bits of iron and granite; although primitive, it could cause serious wounds.

The enemy

The two main groups in Angola were the MPLA and UPA, the *União dos Povos de Angola* guerrilla movement that was renamed in 1961 as the *Frente Nacional de Libertação de Angola* or FNLA. There were several sub-units of rebels but these were gradually absorbed between the two.

There was little love lost between these fighting groups. Both despised the Portuguese, but also fought many pitched battles against each other, which was not surprising since the FNLA was backed by Washington and the MPLA became a Soviet surrogate and later also the Chinese. This demarcation was a feature of the Cold War and was to be found in other African liberation struggles, such as in Rhodesia and South West Africa (later Namibia).

By 1968/9 the MPLA had established itself firmly as the main guerrilla force within Sector D. Yet it also wasted a lot of hardware and men combating the UPA/ FLNA alliance rather than the Portuguese. Quite often this activity extended to MPLA informers indicating to the Portuguese the whereabouts of opposition rebel groups and letting the colonial army eradicate their common enemy.

It was Lisbon that first observed a marked difference between the ability of the MPLA and FNLA in their respective combat roles. The Portuguese viewed the MPLA as "resilient fighters ... tough, wily and dangerous" and clearly eager to win over the 'hearts and minds' of the local population. MPLA men would ask villages for food instead of seizing it, as other cadres often did. Also, the Marxists rarely touched the local women while the pro-West FNLA earned the distrust of many tribal groups by abusing the women of those with whom they were associated.

Early in the war the Portuguese viewed the FNLA as an effective force but by 1969 it had been gradually weakened by lack of discipline.

Insurgent-aligned civilians in Sector D

The guerrillas were supported by between 10,000 and 15,000 African civilians living in the mountainous jungle regions of Sector D who afforded strong support to the insurgents at the start of the war because of genuine loyalty to the cause, tribal allegiance or just plain coercion. They would feed and host groups of fighters passing through on the way south from the Congo, and occasionally secrete them in their villages. The villages, or *sanzalas*, were mostly found in jungle clearings as were their crops. Some remote settlements were large enough to house a field hospital. The staple crop was what it had always been: manioc or cassava root. The root could be planted and left to mature untended. It could be harvested in two months, either by the villagers or by insurgents. They also grew maize and millet and, if time allowed, beans. Meat was rare. If there was grain to spare it was used it to make a fairly potent beer.

'Death walkers': Portuguese foot patrols

Setting: Sector D, Dembos mountains (also Cabinda Enclave, 1969). The insurgents in the Dembos referred to the Portuguese jungle patrols as 'death walkers'. Foot patrols usually ranged from between twenty to thirty soldiers under an officer and three sergeants. Patrols could last three to five days, but Portuguese troops preferred to overnight in the more secure environments.

The men carried everything they needed: food, as much water as was practicable, rifles, usually three machine guns (fore, after and, if possible, in the middle of the strung-out column), ammunition, mortars, one or two vintage bazookas and rockets, a stretcher and a medical kit for the unit's medic.

The group walked in single file, each man trained for specific duties linked to whatever additional weapon or ammunition he hauled. He was trained to perform the

Convoys faced more than the dangers of ambush.

duties of the two men immediately in front and the two behind, so he could take over if they were put out of action. They were trained to know when to take cover because conditions in the jungle under fire made communications difficult because of the heavy tropical foliage. Most time they wouldn't be able to see their officers and, depending on how far strung-out the column was, probably not hear them either.

Patrols walked silently due to the Portuguese boots (canvas with rubber soles) and the rotting vegetation of the jungle floor and most times used sign language to communicate. Even when the squad halted for a meal in a clearing, few soldiers talked and they certainly never smoked in the bush.* A third of the men would be rotationally detached from the main group to stand guard during these breaks.

Black soldiers acted as trackers; they could follow a two-day-old trail through bush and jungle for a further two days. In this way the average patrol could cover something like a hundred kilometres in heavily overgrown jungle in five days, though obviously, if there were major waterways to cross, it would be less. If the patrol was

---

* Conditions in Mozambique became much more lax as the war progressed. As Colonel Ron Reid-Daly, founding commander of the Rhodesian Selous Scouts told me, when he was seconded for a while with the Portuguese Army in Mozambique, some of the soldiers on patrol would talk between themselves and others would smoke, almost as if they were warning the enemy that they were in the area. These issues are dealt with in detail in the author's book *Portugal's Guerrilla Wars in Africa: Lisbon's Three Wars in Angola, Mozambique and Portuguese Guinea.*

Fuzileiros on operations.

following an insurgent trail they would customarily prefer to march alongside the trail to avoid booby traps or anti-personnel mines but this was often impossible in densely foliated terrain. Conditions in grasslands were obviously a lot easier.

Herding civilians

A UPA tactic was to move entire communities of 200 to 8,000 into the jungle; the groups were larger nearer the border with the two Congos. Lisbon appreciated that the tactic damaged the economy because many of those shanghaied might have been working on local plantations. It also provided the insurgents with a ready source of recruits. The civilian men were encouraged to join insurgent ranks while their women stayed behind to raise crops, which would feed other groups of fighters passing through. This tactic was particularly effective in 1963/64 and Angola suffered a severe coffee shortage despite the fact there was a world glut.

Once on the move it would sometimes take several weeks for a rebel group to cross the border. The Portuguese army, aware of the implications, would task the air force to try to spot insurgent columns and stopper groups would be deployed to halt them.

A rebel group constantly on the move faced numerous issues, including a shortage of food. There were many reports of desperate abductees having to resort to eating the grass around their campsites. In contrast, their insurgent guards usually had enough to eat. They tended to shoot stragglers who were unable to keep pace with the main bunch. The Portuguese could often tell the location of a convoy by the presence of circling vultures. If they dropped commandos ahead of the column, forcing it to 'bombshell', the insurgents would melt into the bush to look for other civilians groups to help them.

Civilians were often moved into Congo-Leo (later Congo-Kinshasa). One guerrilla claim put the number of abductees in the region at about half a million by 1965, though this is unlikely because the region would never have been able to support such numbers. Some of these people went on to join the rebels, others attempted to return to Angola after they arrived. Self-appointed bands of armed youths (*jeunesse*) patrolled the borders and shot anybody they found trying to return. Eventually about two-third of abductees managed to return home. Over time the Portuguese began to feed and house returning refugees and place them in Malayan Emergency-style 'protected villages' or *aldeamentos*.

Insurgent accuracy

From the start of the war, the Portuguese considered the majority of insurgents inadequately trained, or possibly because most were illiterate, unable to comprehend the nature and complexities of modern insurgency warfare. For a start, rebel shooting was poor, a common problem in Third World conflicts of that period, with the single exception of Vietnam. The average rebel could rarely hit anything beyond a hundred metres. The same applied to the use of mortars: fire was rarely delivered square on target. Weapons' handling improved markedly with the use of the Soviet RPG-2, and thereafter the more advanced RPG-7.

Rebels excelled in the mine-laying techniques. Over time this was to become the single biggest bugbear facing Portuguese forces in Africa and played a significant role in lowering morale among government troops. It is worth mentioning that in line with Viet Cong routines in South East Asia, insurgents in the Dembos were expected to collect their spent cartridges. They were not issued with fresh ammunition unless they were able to present the shells of expended cartridges back at camp. This was seen as proof that they'd been involved in combat.

Insurgent attacks on Portuguese camps

Most insurgent attacks on Portuguese camps in Sector D took place after dark. However, by 1969 the insurgents were conducting mock attacks during the day. These were intended to bring the Portuguese officers into the open where insurgent snipers would target them. Portuguese officers soon learned to discard anything designating rank on their uniforms.

Insurgent ambush in the mountains

Road convoys were particularly vulnerable in the Dembos mountains. The roads, as we have seen, were bad and the insurgents active. A typical ambush by insurgents in the mountainous Dembos: the rebels would choose a stretch of road with clear visibility for some distance in both directions, in a valley or on a rise overlooking the road or track. If the area was overgrown they would attack from above, firing down onto the convoy. This offered a better opportunity of escape once the action was complete. The standard Portuguese response was to brake hard, jump from the vehicles and dash for cover on the side of the road, into elephant grass or shrubbery, while firing their rifles. Early in the war the insurgents often positioned men with machetes—*catanas*—alongside the road and the Portuguese would usually fire into suspect areas at random, quite often with requisite results.

Ambush on the Terreiro road

One ambush that took place involved two Portuguese army jeeps early in the day travelling out of Terreiro, Sector F. The occupants were Captain de Campos, driving the lead vehicle and with seven of his men in total. An insurgent group of perhaps twenty rebels had set up positions on a rise commanding a section of road that went around the foot of a hill through a dip. It lay about thirty metres above the road and provided the attackers with excellent visibility in both directions. The area had patches of jungle interspersed with elephant grass along the road with a three-metre-deep gully between the road and the insurgent positions, but obscured by long grass. The rebels had also taken the trouble to cut an escape path through the nearby jungle.

The road was good with the Portuguese driving fast to ensure they did the round trip before lunch. Captain de Campos recounts: "We came round one of the many bends, fairly close to town. As we turned sharply and dropped into a dip, they opened fire from a position above us. It was obviously a good spot and the attack took us all completely by surprise." Campos's men went through the drills and ended up on the far side of their attackers, their position partially hidden by foliage and elephant grass. Once there, they returned fire. One man in the second jeep was badly wounded in the gut and the captain decided on decisive action. Some of the men who could see the captain were given hand signals to hurl grenades, the others concentrating their fire on the enemy position above. They followed that up with a hell-bent charge and more grenades but were slowed by the gully. Once past this obstacle the insurgents began to withdraw, leaving behind one dead.

Ambush of a commando patrol

A commando captain was leading a patrol of twenty men. In an operation in thick bush, the captain tripped an anti-personnel explosive improvised from a mortar

Right: Portuguese troops in the Dembos.

Below: A PAF Puma picking up troops.

bomb and lost both legs below the knee. The insurgents followed up with RPGs, mortars, grenades and machine guns. Despite blood loss and intermittently losing consciousness, the captain retained control of his men until the enemy withdrew. The unit suffered thirteen casualties—five killed and eight wounded, two critically— which was exceptionally high compared to normal contacts in the bush. The captain subsequently won the highest military honour in Lisbon.

Encountering an enemy sanzala in the jungle

When a Portuguese patrol discovered a *sanzala*, an encampment, in the jungle, usually after dark, the decision was immediate, having been rehearsed in training many times before. If the patrol believed there might be enemy in the camp, they would go through several steps that usually assured a measure of success.

First, the officer would signal by hand for his men to freeze. He would send forward two or three of his scouts with good experience in knife-handling to eliminate any sentries[*] and reconnoitre the immediate surrounds[**] The team needed to establish enemy strength and where dispersed, best approaches and possible dangers. They also had to identify potential machine-gun positions so as to allow for the requisite 'killing zones', the fields of fire or the lines beyond which the Portuguese soldiers could not go in order to avoid 'friendly fire'. That established, and their presence still not revealed, the scouts would return to the main section. Watches were synchronized and final instructions given, after which two machine-gun teams were allowed five or ten minutes to establish a crossfire zone. Each machine-gun team was led by one of the scouts to the previously identified position, usually on opposite sides of the *sanzala*. The others spread out. At the predetermined time all sections would simultaneously attack. A flanking movement would provide additional fire into the 'killing zone'.

'Rehabilitation'

During the course of the Angolan war, captured insurgents were most times offered a simple choice: join the Portuguese army in its efforts to destroy their comrades,

---

[*] The Portuguese thought the insurgent sentries were better than theirs, or at least better than the metropolitan soldiers. Africans born in the jungle—on both sides of the conflict—were thoroughly familiar with the 'early-warning systems' of the jungle. The Africans could hear a whisper at fifty metres and a cough at almost a kilometre. The animals in the jungle could sense a larger animal like a human nearby and go quiet; this produced an eerie and unnatural silence and both sides would immediately be made aware that something was up.

[**] The insurgents didn't just camp out in the jungle without taking elaborate precautions, so surrounding the *sanzala* was often difficult and sometimes almost impossible. The insurgents variably located their camps to exploit some or other natural advantage, such as a formidable jungle 'wall' on two sides, or perhaps on a bend along a river or next to a steep hill. It was actually quite rare to take an enemy encampment completely by surprise.

or else ... which meant the man was expected to disclose to his captors everything he experienced while with the guerrilla force, from the day he was recruited up to the present time. If the response was satisfactory (and it often was not) the captive would then be required to lead a combat squad through the jungle to the hideouts he and his fellow guerrillas had frequented. Or he might accompany the army in an attack on his former base, or possibly, a more distant headquarters. Clearly, his role with government troops would have been observed by his former compadres and there would be little chance of him rejoining his old unit should he try to do so. By 1969 there were about a thousand former insurgents fighting for the Portuguese in Angola. Their role was much valued because, as one officer commented, "they know the jungle; they know the enemy and, most important of all, they know every ruse of the native."

Imbu was one of the young men whom the author met at Nambuangongo and was a good example. He was captured by the Portuguese following a firefight on 18 March 1967 after he had been wounded in a guerrilla attack on a coffee farm. He chose to join the Portuguese and led them to his former camp where several of his erstwhile comrades were killed. Imbu subsequently became a section and was nominated for a decoration for his part in destroying an insurgent supply column in which he killed two men himself. I was told by his former commanding officer that Imbu was killed a year later in an ambush.

Attack on Vila Teixeira de Sousa

Insurgents attacked Vila Teixeira de Sousa on the railway line in the east of Angola at lunchtime on Christmas Day 1968. The entire garrison had just been seated for an elaborate lunch when the assault started. The enemy first attacked the African quarter of town, giving the Portuguese time to take up defensive positions. For the loss of only a few defenders, black and white, the Portuguese killed more than 300 attackers.

2. WHAT WENT ON IN PORTUGAL'S AFRICAN WARS

Hostilities in Angola on the Atlantic coast of Africa were very different from what was taking place in Mozambique which lies on the Indian Ocean. Lisbon won the day in Angola but was finally defeated by domestic politics back home.

The third colony where Portugal was fighting a colonial war was Portuguese Guinea. There the guerrillas were powerfully motivated: better organized, more compact as a fighting force and geographically, the PAIGC (African Party for the Independence of Guinea and Cape Verde) had the advantage of size because the country they fought for was tiny, about half the size of minuscule Latvia. Also, Lisbon's forces in Guinea faced neighbours hostile to everything for which that European nation stood: the Marxist Republic of Guinea to the south and east, with Senegal to its immediate north. Almost with impunity, the guerrillas were able to run in and out of both countries during the course of hostilities.

By way of comparison, Mozambique eventually became a much less intense guerrilla insurgency: it was a war where distance played into the hands of the defenders. The capital, Lourenço Marques, was more than 2,500 kilometres from the country's northern frontier with Tanzania and much of the hardware the rebels needed for their war effort had to be brought south either on bicycles, the occasional truck or on the backs of villagers who either volunteered for the task or were pressganged. Things changed to the advantage of the guerrillas not long after Zambia, headed by President Kenneth Kaunda, entered the fray. That happened following his country being granted independence by Britain in October 1964. It took only weeks for a new front to be opened along Mozambique's western regions, adjacent to the freshly independent Malawi (until July 1964 Nyasaland, a country with little stomach for guerrilla struggles). Suddenly Lisbon was faced with a two-front campaign on the littoral of the Indian Ocean.

The operational core of Portugal's war efforts in Africa consequently rested largely on its single and most valuable historical asset which was colonial Angola. A huge country, it was blessed with a permanent-resident settler community that had put roots down centuries before. Indeed, the majority of its citizens regarded Angola as home because they knew no other. It is worth mentioning that as hostilities progressed, there was a significant section of that settler community talking about possibly seceding from Lisbon's control and declaring itself independent, as Brazil had done almost a century and a half before and colonial British Rhodesia was to do in November 1965. Moreover, these people—of all races—were prepared to fight in

Early press photo of guerrillas undergoing training.

order to maintain the dominance they had regained after those tenuous early days in 1961. They had the singular advantage that their enemy was fragmented between several warring factions, never mind that the country was—and still is—potentially one of the wealthiest on the African continent. In the words of one American investor who has been quoted often enough: "Angola has diamonds, gold and enough iron ore and manganese to keep China happy for a century. Then there are hardwoods, a grain basket in the interior highlands, coffee, cocoa, as well as a string of other commodities ... wealth galore!" After oil was discovered in the north, even with the ongoing conflict, things there were actually looking up.

One of the most significant problems facing Lisbon in those early stages of the insurrection was the lack of modern weapons. When hostilities started in 1961 the Portuguese forces were poorly equipped to cope with the everyday demands of a major modern counterinsurgency. It had been standard procedure, up to that point, to send obsolete military hardware to the African colonies, while all the good stuff was retained for NATO use. Thus, the first military operations in Angola were conducted using antiquated German cast-off rifles, some of which dated back to before the turn of the century.

Communications was another issue: almost all the radio sets available when hostilities kicked off were of World War II vintage. With such shortcomings, Lisbon obviously needed to act: the government did not need to be told that if their commanders could not communicate with their troops in the field, they were lost.

As a result, various companies like Siemens and Philips were commissioned to provide the necessary. Interestingly, South Africa, sensing that the Portuguese wars were

Early days of the conflict with paratroopers preparing for a jump. (Revista Militar)

not going well and that things might turn sour along its own frontiers with Black Africa, soon followed suit with much attention devoted to better communications and, notably, electronic intelligence (ELINT).

We deal with weapons in some detail a little later. Let it be said at this stage, that though there were many initial hiccups, the Portuguese army did manage to pull its chestnuts out of the fire though it took a lot of casualties in the process.

From the earliest days of the uprising, the war in Angola was always at its most intense in the huge and undeveloped region that lay to the north of Luanda. This was a remote, heavily foliaged coffee-growing and tropical hardwood area and farms were sparse and isolated, which was why the rebels could make so much headway to begin with.[*]

The first time I was able to accompany an aerial supply drop—handled by a bulky Noratlas transporter—we took off from Luanda International Airport and dropped our cargo by parachute onto a mountain strongpoint barely fifteen minutes' flying time out of the capital. That surprised me. Until then, I (and a lot of others) had been

---

[*] Al J. Venter, *Portugal's Guerrilla Wars in Africa: Lisbon's Three Wars in Angola, Mozambique and Portuguese Guinea.*

led to believe that hostilities were taking place somewhere adjacent to the Congolese frontier, which was hundreds of kilometres farther north. But then, it was in the interests of Lisbon's high command to remain vague about most things related to the war.

When we finally put down in Sector D/ Comsec D at Santa Eulalia, a good deal of the country to the north of the camp—which stretched away toward the west and the coast—was either jungle or swamp. Indeed, this was an exceedingly grim environment in which to wage war. Being an equatorial tropical region, there were rivers everywhere. There were also numerous bridges that, in turn, had been blown, first by the retreating Portuguese and then, government forces having gained the upper hand, once more by the rebels. That, in the minds of many observers suggested a measure of unexpected sophistication and possibly foreign involvement, which was also mentioned off the record during subsequent briefings.

With time, the Portuguese rebuilt many of those bridges, because movement into the interior without them would have been impossible. Obviously the engineers doing that work had to be protected, which resulted in blockhouses dominating high points all over the place and, of course needing still more men on the ground to protect them.

One of the first things to happen after I arrived at the base was a briefing by the unit intelligence officer. It was pretty straightforward but, as I was to discover as our fact-finding tour progressed, it was also spliced with occasional bits of disinformation. As the saying goes, the first casualty in war is truth.

With about two dozen trucks and a helicopter or two on hand for emergencies— these aircraft always operated out of Luanda and were never permanently stationed in the interior because the unit was often mortared—the camp garrison was reasonably mobile. Like several other Portuguese army units in the region, the army's main task—apart from running convoys—was to protect the local African population.

The camp at Santa Eulalia was quite compact, with its own clinic, surgical theatre as well as a fully functioning dental unit. Soldiers farther afield who needed more advanced treatment, such as root canal treatment or an appendectomy, were flown into the camp by light aircraft or helicopter. But for that to happen it needed good notice because Portugal's air assets were always sparse. More serious casualties were airlifted to the military hospital in Luanda, usually on special litters fitted in a single-engine aircraft. Or they would be flown out by helicopter, which landed on a concrete slab behind the clinic that was used after hours as a tennis court by the officers. Clearly, this was a lot more than the insurgents had to offer their male and female fighters. Which was something else to emerge during the course of the briefings: there were many more female combatants in guerrilla ranks than most observers realized.

The session at Santa Eulalia lasted well into the evening and was initially handled by a baby-faced lieutenant with his left arm in a sling. His shoulder had been 'creased' by an AK bullet in an ambush the week before, we were told. "It could have

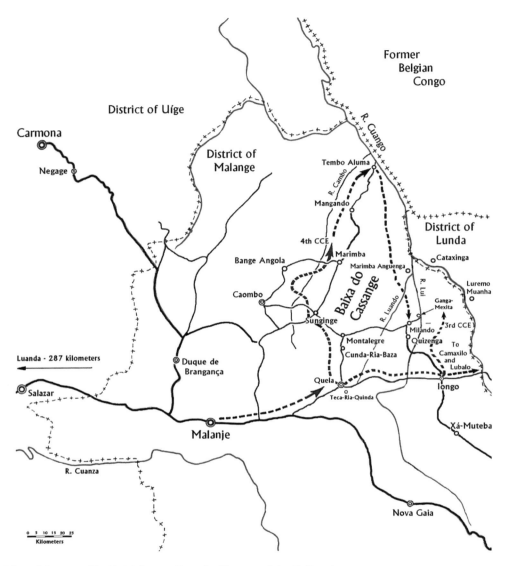

Map of the guerrillas' initial area of revolt. (Courtesy John P. Cann)

been worse," the youthful officer admitted: "we were caught in an ambush in some bush country and the bullet ricocheted off the gun turret on board the Panhard I'd commandeered as a command post ... I'd been on a routine convoy run south of here."

In fairly good English he elaborated on some of the problems faced by Comsec D Command. The enemy, he told us, came into northern Angola from an area along the Congo frontier, roughly peaking between Matadi (the Congo's only major port

One of the first photos to emerge of dead insurgents killed in early retaliatory raids.

with access to the ocean) and Kinshasa, the Congo's capital or, as it had been known before, Leopoldville.

He explained that many of the rebels also entered Angola from the former French colony, Congo-Brazzaville. "They cross the river at night in shallow-bottomed *pirogues* [dugout canoes] and though we had problems in the past, naval patrols have been quite successful in stopping some, but not all these infiltrators. If you've seen the river, you'll know that the Congo is wide—many kilometres across in places. Also, there are thousands of floating islands constantly carried downstream by the current.

"So it's actually quite easy to hide in those matted reed or papyrus islands when you see the lights of a patrol craft approaching. And frankly, it's physically impossible to inspect them all ... that would need thousands more men," the officer opined. Once over the border, it took the average insurgent moving over incredibly difficult terrain that included often impenetrable tropical jungle, mountains, fast-flowing rivers that sometimes disappeared into swampland that stretch all the way across to the horizon, about six weeks to reach Sector D. Just getting there, he admitted, was an achievement.

In retrospect, it was comparatively easy for insurgent groups to infiltrate Portuguese territory from the Congo in the early days. There were half a dozen or more Portuguese administrative or customs posts located close to the unmarked demarcation line and still more a few dozen kilometres behind it. The distance between the Noqui and Cuango frontier posts for instance, was roughly 400 kilometres so, calculations apart, there were any number of places where the rebels could cut through and head south. In fact, it left large tracts of territory open and unprotected and even as hostilities continued with Portuguese army patrols doing their best to control movement, clandestine crossings were an everyday event.

We were shown our position on a map of the area. Pinpointed were other camps in Sector D—Zala to the north, Zemba lying farther toward the south and then the pivotal crossroads settlement of Nambuangongo slap bang in the middle. There were four other Portuguese military bases in an area probably half the size of Switzerland, each responsible for the security of quite large sectors.

Nambuangongo, he told us, was probably the most interesting of all because it came with a history that went back to the earliest days of the war. 'Nambu', as the troops liked to call it, had been the original headquarters of the rebel army in Angola. They'd taken it by force, killed everybody there, including a number of logging people whose families had taken refuge at the home of the local *chefe do posto*, to no avail. Captured victims were fed lengthwise into industrial circular saws in the logging plants, the local political administrator included. This was something the rebels boasted about quite openly in Congolese bars when they returned on furlough and was put out in several news reports that reached Europe by Agence France Presse.[*]

Fighting in the vicinity of his base, the lieutenant recalled, had not only been fierce, but consistent. It had been that way since mid-1961, he explained.

At which point another officer, Captain Ramos de Campos, took over and told us that the guerrillas still tried to retake the hilltop base from time to time. They had apparently come close to doing so several times, he reckoned, especially when numbers of troops normally based there were away, either on patrol or doing convoy duties.

It was at Nambuangongo that the rebels had achieved some of their best successes. Their political commissars would talk about "our most glorious victories against the Fascist colonial forces", an expression regularly espoused by the guerrilla radio station broadcasting from Brazzaville. Apart from terminology, said de Campos, you couldn't really scoff at that notion, because early on, they'd actually brushed aside everything the government could muster at short notice, all the way to the outskirts of Luanda. In fact, he confided, there was a period of several months in the early days when "those people" were masters of just about all they surveyed, "But no longer ... these days we have a pretty solid grip on things, but that doesn't mean that we can sit back." He explained that it was integral to the insurgent masterplan to recapture Nambuangongo, "and snatching it from out under us again would be regarded as a most significant victory. So they keep on trying". He was frank that were that to happen, it would be an enormous defeat.

---

[*]   Bernardo Teixeira, with an introduction by Robert Ruark, *The Fabric of Terror: Three Days in Angola*.

Portuguese troops embarking at Lisbon for Africa.

Another officer at the briefing was Captain Virgil Magalhan. His job was to outline guerrilla tactics, which was when he called for a display board to be brought into the command centre.

Using a pointer, he detailed how the war had entered a new phase involving land-mines and the types of attacks being launched. He explained how the insurgents liked to lay their ambushes, the types of weapons with which they were equipped—all of Soviet origin, including RPG-2s—and where their main bases were situated. The sector was experiencing about four or five actions a week, he said. Most were ambushes and some were quite heavy and invariably resulted in casualties. As opposed to the early days of the invasion when the rebels attacked in groups often 200 strong, they tended to concentrate in smaller groups of about twenty or less at the time of our visit.

Also notable was the fact that some of the insurgents had been trained outside Angola. Some had spent time, often years, behind the Iron Curtain and could speak fluent Russian. Others trained in Eastern Europe could master German, Bulgarian or Czech "and a fat lot of use that is in this jungle," he joked. "As for ability, they're a mixed bag, which actually holds for most of Africa's so-called liberation wars,' he suggested.

"The majority of fighters are indifferent, reasonably well-trained, but lacking in either focus or purpose. That said, their section leaders can sometimes be pretty

Luanda in 1960 was a delightful, bustling city, Africa's Rio some called it.

good when it comes to tactics and the use of the more advanced weapons like heavy machine guns, rocket-propelled grenades or mortars. The balance, thankfully, are dismal. They've been taught, and that's about it." He reckoned that things could change, radically perhaps, but that was the situation at the time.

It was notable that in spite of the threat, Portuguese officers—in all three services—quite often displayed rank on their uniforms in the various operational areas. With the threat of attack omnipresent, especially in the bush, one would have thought they might have discarded their epaulettes and gold braid, or at least used muted shades which would have made it difficult to distinguish who was who from a distance, very much as other Western military forces do in hostile areas. But that was not always the case. Granted, they became incognito on patrol or while on convoy duty, but by then, the insurgents knew exactly who was in charge because they were the ones issuing commands. Additionally, the insurgents had their own means of monitoring activity in Portuguese military bases. No doubt they used some of the domestic African staff as informers; it had always been the African way.

There was a good deal of speculation about the kind of training received by the insurgents. This was a consistent theme in most of the operational sectors. The perception among the majority of Portuguese troops was that as enemy, the guerrillas were an inferior element, though to this outsider, that did not make sense considering

In the first months of the war most retaliatory actions were improvised.

the number of troops the rebels had succeeded in tying down. The argument applied as much to basic tactics as to accurately firing their weapons. In truth, it was a fundamental misconception that had obviously cost lives in the past, for while the ability of the majority of African guerrillas was nothing to shout about, there were some brilliant and innovative combatants within their ranks.[*]

Nino—later General Nino who was later to become president of Guiné-Bissau—was among them. He successfully countered the Portuguese army in a succession of military operations in that distant enclave, including the series of island battles on the offshore archipelago that included Como where some of the bitterest fighting took place.

The common denominator among them all was that in the choice of weapons the insurgents preferred the tried and trusted AK-47. Functional under all conditions and ubiquitous, it was the weapon of choice among most revolutionary armies in Africa and it is still that way today. It was notable that apart from AKs—and squad weapons such as RPDs, RPKs as well as ageing Simonovs—Soviet-manufactured rifles have always taken the lead. Yet, almost consistently, the guerrillas lost more of their own men in action than did the Portuguese because they were not using their weapons to good effect. Even though they might initially have had the advantage of surprise in an ambush, it was the same almost each time there was a contact: the Kalashnikov would be put on full automatic and firing would continue for a couple of seconds until the magazine was empty with most shots going high.

---

[*]   John P. Cann, *Counterinsurgency in Africa: The Portuguese Way of War, 1961–1974.*

One of the first retaliatory actions in Angola, with a Panhard armoured car in the background. (Manuel Alves)

The age-old guerrilla tactic of blocking roads with felled trees.

Nonetheless, the insurgents would work to a series of systems that had strong Soviet overtones: almost everything was done by the book. They would choose a stretch of road with good visibility for some distance in both directions and if the area was heavily foliated, they'd attack from a position above the road, firing down onto the convoy. This, as we have seen, would give them the edge, with escape invariably the immediate prerogative. As with the Rhodesian bush war and sub-sequently with the South Africans in their conflict in northern South West Africa (present-day Namibia) there was a perpetual fear of helicopter gunships among the

The Portuguese army parades along Luanda's seafront, the Marginal. (Revista Militar)

rebels. Even if they did manage to cause serious damage, they'd rarely hang about and finish the job.

The rebel army in northern Angola by the time I arrived in Sector D was estimated at about 6,000 regulars. Their numbers were more preponderant than the strength of the Portuguese army, though with conscription back home having taken effect, things had improved. Apart from the insurgents, there were two or three times that number of African civilians who lived in the jungles and among the mountains of the sector, many caught in the perennial crosshairs of conflict. While not part of the regular insurgent movement, civilians did tend to provide the rebels with useful support when needed, customarily acting as porters or bearers. They'd also be tasked with taking out the dead and tending the wounded in their villages if the casualty could not be hauled back to their own lines.

The majority might have been innocent bystanders to start with, but that was no longer the case. Early rebel successes had given many of these tribal people the desire for more of the same, often as a result of tribal associations or simply because they were sympathetic to what the guerrillas referred to as a just cause.

It was interesting that though guerrilla medics were hardly sophisticated in their approach and most times ill-equipped, they did save a lot of lives because there were more than a few foreign doctors who crossed the border from the north to help the cause. They came from all over the world, some from African countries, others from Cuba, China and even Vietnam, with one officer adding that the bulk of guerrilla medical supplies—which covered a huge range of drugs and equipment—came largely from Europe, much of it from Scandinavia as well as Canada.

3. THE LAND WAR

For Portugal's President Antonio de Salazar's *estado novo* (new state) the mainte-nance and retention of the country's African territories—the *Ultramar*—was the key goal. The loss of Brazil in 1822 had cut deeply into Lusitanian pride and the start of the war in Angola in 1961 was a matter of supreme national interest. Angola was the jewel in the crown, the wealthiest and the most productive of the three African colonial territories. With the discovery of offshore oil in the north of the country, it was already regarded as a future powerhouse of the nation's wealth.

Of course, it helped that five families controlled the extractive industries in Angola, Mozambique, and Guinea-Bissau, and their activities were key to Salazar's economic strategy.

For all that, Lisbon's African wars very soon began to haemorrhage the country's finances and conditions were not helped by thousands of would-be conscripts and serving members of the armed forces deserting.

Once Lisbon accepted that it was in for the long haul in Angola—the Mozambique insurgency only happened a few years later—Portugal wasted no time at all in mod-ernizing its armed forces. From West Germany it acquired the production licence for the G3, a NATO 7.62-calibre rifle developed after World War II by Heckler & Koch in conjunction with the Spanish agency SETME. That weapon replaced the antiquated

Alouette IIIs
dusting off.

Mauser Karabiner, and just in time because the revolt in the disputed north of Angola had almost spiralled out of control. Some Belgian Fabrique Nationale FALs as well as American Armalite AR-10s were acquired for Special Forces airborne use until a collapsible-stock version of the all-purpose G3 became available.

There was an obvious need for sub-machine guns (mainly by officers in select units, cavalry as well as reserve, paramilitary units and state security forces). Israeli Uzis, the Austrian Steyr MP 34 m/942 and the Portuguese FBP m/948 were the adopted weapons for this role.

For light machine guns, Portugal first approached Britain for its all-purpose GPMG but that requested was declined. The Mauser MG 42 machine gun was issued until 1968 when another Heckler & Koch variation, the HK-1, came into production and was made available to forces fighting in the colonies. Support weapons included outdated American bazookas, as well as standard NATO 60mm and 81mm mortars. These were later supplemented by 120mm mortars and howitzers.

There was a good deal of improvisation as the wars progressed. Though the Portuguese army had limited supplies of the 3.5-inch M20 rocket launcher, they initially lacked an answer to the Soviet RPG-2 that was supplied to all guerrilla forces by the Soviets. So they designed their own bazooka, called the *Lança Granadas Fogute*. This was a 37mm bazooka-type device designed by Cesare Dante Vacchi, an Italian commando veteran who had seen action in several wars, including Algeria and who

The surprisingly effective bazooka device home-produced by the Portuguese. It fired a 37mm air-to-ground SNEB rocket.

ended up in the ranks of Lisbon's commandos. Appropriately called the 'Dante', it fired the 37mm French SNEB air-to-ground rocket and became much favoured among those to whom it was issued, *comandos Africanos* units especially. It proved so successful under combat conditions that the Portuguese soon manufactured a variant of Vacchi's prototype: all aluminium and much lighter than the American bazooka.

Portugal faced numerous problems in trying to acquire modern weapons and aircraft. It became progressively more difficult to buy heavier matériel to counter the kind supplied to the rebels by the Soviets. In fact it was Lisbon's NATO allies who were the most reticent in supplying hardware for use in the colonial campaigns, despite Portuguese acquisition attempts going as far back as 1957. For all these reasons, South African support became increasingly indispensable, and, as I was told by General Bettencourt Rodrigues, impossible to resist, despite Salazar's traditional reservations regarding Pretoria's hegemonic intentions in southern Africa.

Mobile ground operations usually consisted of patrol sweeps by armoured car and reconnaissance vehicles. Several armoured cars were used. There was the GMC Fox which was basically a modified Humber IV manufactured in Canada. The main difference was the fitting of a .50-calibre machine gun, which replaced the 37mm gun. These armoured cars were progressively replaced by Panhard AML-60s from the

mid-1960s on as well as EBR (Fox) armoured cars. Some heavier equipment went onto the Panhards (fitted with an H-60 turret and armed with twin 7.62 mm machine guns on the left together with a single 60mm mortar on the right). In later stages, the Portuguese-built *Bravia Chaimite* became operational, an eleven-man armoured personnel carrier (APC) with a .50 Browning mounted on the turret.

Though deployed mostly in urban security duties, Daimler Dingos, small, two-man armoured scout cars were always in the background during official parades, some used in convoy support roles when needed.

There were numerous other changes implemented, largely of necessity. Confronted by a rapidly improving guerrilla force, Lisbon's ground, sea and air forces were gradually reorganized to slot into a newly configured counterinsurgency role, with new units such as the *comandos Africanos* that emerged early

A grim side to the Angolan war was the consequences of a landmine blast.

in the war as well as the *Fuzileiros*, upgraded into the tough and sophisticated all-purpose marine combat element they became.

The nature of so many of these changes is still to be seen within the Portuguese armed forces today, with numerous Special Forces units doing regular service in many of the world's trouble spots, including Afghanistan, the Central African Republic and, most prominently, against AQIM—al-Qaeda in the Islamic Maghreb—in West Africa.

When the African crisis first broke, Portugal found itself ill-equipped for a series of sudden and unexpected developments. A poor nation with a small population, the last thing Salazar needed was a war far thousands of kilometres from its native shores with the country's international transport system woefully inadequate. Captive markets had not produced the bonanza that Salazar's economic theories predicted, and colonial subsidies now began to cripple the treasury, even without the added expense of combat. There was little spare cash for armaments and not enough manpower for domestic needs as well as the army. Also, it was hardly a secret that the dictatorship was not popular—either in Europe or in the United States—so no extraordinary aid could be looked for from either quarter even though a lot of US aviation assets ended up doing good work in Angola and the French did rally with their Alouette helicopters which had to be paid for in cash (as well as a couple of squadrons of Pumas at a later stage).

Yet aid for the insurgents, as it transpired, was plentiful, given the newly independent African states that now surrounded Portuguese colonies and the readiness of communist countries to supply arms to insurgent movements. The international community was actually falling over itself to cosy up to a couple of dozen newly independent African countries, many of which saw Europe and the US as a source of almost unlimited largesse.

The invasion of Angola in 1961 was hardly a major incursion: the problem basically was that the security forces were not militarily prepared. With the rebels flooding in, the focus of attention was fixed on the international Congolese border in the São Salvador and the Dembos areas. Many rebels were of Bakongo tribal origin from outside Angola and, as it was discovered later, the majority had never heard of Holden Roberto. But they were firm about their objectives, of which there were four:

- Drive the whites out of Angola in the same way that the Belgians had been forced to quit the Congo the year before.
- Coerce the indigenous population to participate in the struggle.
- Incite racial hatred between whites and blacks.
- Attract international attention and, as a result, possible United Nation intervention.

Among rebel groups there was some preplanning but very little within Angola itself. The revolutionaries had the single advantage of being able to dominate the jungle

Portuguese paratroopers advance to assault.

terrain of the target area which offered them good cover, with the mobility of the Portuguese forces severely limited, exacerbated by the fact that they arrived at the end of the rainy season when many of the roads were still impassable.

The greatest number of non-insurgent deaths occurred over just two days, the 15 and 16 March: whites, *mesticos* and blacks were slaughtered, most times indiscriminately with between 200 and 300 whites murdered on the first day. *Mestico, assimilado* and Ovimbundu contract labourers were also targeted and anybody who resisted or were not welcoming to these exceedingly brutal savages were summarily executed or mutilated, including Bakongo and Mbundu villagers.

For all this, not everybody made tracks. Some people, both white and black, stayed to defend their homes. The Ovimbundu contract labourers were particularly noted for their loyalty to their employers but most of the others fled. Most settlers made a dash for Luanda from where many flew back to Portugal. They were followed by some Africans, but the majority crossed into the Congo in bids to seek succour among about 200,000 refugees who were already there, with only a handful of dispossessed Portuguese settlers among them. Official Portuguese sources divided the UPA uprising of 1961 into three phases:

1. From 15 March: Terror campaigns by small gangs of poorly armed groups against farms and isolated settlements; property was not damaged as it was promised to UPA supporters. Roads were blocked by felled trees and bridges damaged to limit retaliatory movement. These were all plans formulated in the Congo prior to the invasion.

2. Beginning 5 April. There were mass attacks on larger settlements and military posts by slightly better armed groups who were said to be under the influence of drugs and aided by witchdoctors. Destruction of the coffee crop was the key objective, with farms, buildings and machinery also destroyed.

3. Following Portuguese reoccupation in subsequent months. Small, mobile and well-armed guerrilla groups conducted guerrilla warfare including hit-and-run assaults on military and other targets, a situation that continued until the end of the war thirteen years later.

Guerrilla war supplies came from many sources, though the bulk of it was Soviet. China ended up sending regular cargos of military hardware to the Angolan rebels, much of it channelled through Dar es Salaam harbour on Africa's east coast. Other nations that supplied weapons included just about every Eastern Bloc state, Cuba, Egypt, Ethiopia (that of necessity was developing a modest arms industry), Yugoslavia with its landmines and anti-aircraft weapons and more, all good quality matériel, though several other countries were eager to offload surplus stock only if paid for in cash.

Certainly the most destructive of all weapons deployed by Lisbon's insurgent enemies was the landmine, both anti-tank and anti-personnel, an issue that comes prominently to

A flimsy bridge across across the Lue river in northern Angola.

Much of the equipment used by government forces dated from World War II, including early radio sets. (Revista Militar)

the fore within these pages. Lisbon spent years and substantial funds trying to develop effective anti-mining counter-measures but somehow nothing adequate materialized though there were prototypes and test machines galore. The problem, in part, lay with the Portuguese system of control: too many bureaucratic obstacles, too many loops, as it were, for the technicians and functionaries involved with production to jump through. This was peculiar because even tiny Rhodesia was able to come up with several reasonably effective mine-detecting vehicles. Nor did it did take South Africa very long to develop a variety of anti-landmine vehicles, the most prominent being the Rhino, Casspir, Buffel, Ratel and the Mamba among others, some still in service today in places where landmines are a threat, among them the Middle East and Afghanistan.

For Lisbon, the consequence of this debilitating inadequacy was felt by all ground forces for the duration of the three wars and though there has been some dispute about numbers, more Portuguese soldiers became casualties from mines than any other weapon deployed by the guerrillas. The effect on morale among the defenders was obviously severe.

As the war progressed, the MPLA and Portuguese Guinea's PAIGC—as well as FRELIMO in Mozambique—became masters of the arcane skills linked to laying booby traps, something imparted with vigour by many of the Vietcong sappers spotted in rebel ranks from time to time but employed principally in sharing their skills during training.

On the kinds of squad weapons issued to the various guerrilla armies, the AK-47 was obviously to the fore. Others of Soviet origin were the Mosin-Nagent rifle, the SKS carbine and in earlier days, the PPsH sub-machine gun. RPD and PKM machine guns soon also became a feature of conflicts in Africa.

Portuguese troops were tough and resilient in the bush. (Photo Revista Militar)

Support weapons included Soviet and Chinese mortars, the B-10 recoilless rifle as well as the 122mm Katyusha rocket system that, while dated—it was extensively used by the Soviets in World War II—was much favoured by the insurgents because it made a lot of noise. Anti-aircraft weapons included a variety of guns, some multi-barrelled in the 12.7mm and 14.5mm range. With time the Soviet ZU-23, a towed 23mm twin-barrelled auto-cannon became prominent (but mainly in rear-echelon bases because it was heavy and difficult to move about in bush or jungle terrain where roads were few). Several Portuguese air force planes took hits from all these heavy machine guns and some were brought down.

While the authorities tended to claim that the most effective anti-aircraft weapon deployed by the guerrillas was the Strela-2 missile, listed by NATO as the SAM-7 Grail, first introduced by the Soviets to guerrilla forces in Portuguese Guinea in 1973 and in Mozambique the following year, this is open to question. At least two Fiat G.91 fighter-jets were shot down in Guinea and other aircraft took hits from SAMs, but few Portuguese planes were lost to missiles during the course of all three wars. At least two, possibly three 'Dakota' C-47 Skytrains—the American 'Gooney Bird'—in the Portuguese and the South African air forces took MANPAD hits but were still able to make it back to their bases.

The land forces active in forces in Angola constituted the Military Region of Angola (RMA) of the Portuguese army (named Third Military Region' until 1962). The overall entity was foreseen to have included five subordinate regional territorial commands, but these were never activated.

The disposition of the army units in the province at the beginning of the conflict had originally been established in 1953, at a time when no internal conflicts were anticipated in Angola. Portugal's major military concerns at the time were vested in a potential conventional war in Europe against the Warsaw Pact. The organization of

To recapture Nambuangongo from the rebels, armour had to be sent north. (Revista Militar)

the country's colonial military forces before 1961 was based largely on company-sized units scattered across Angola, performing internal security duties. Their role was very much along conventional lines, with army units centred on three infantry regiments as well as several battalion-sized units concentrated in the major urban centres. The idea was that if a global war was launched, NATO would be at the core of it and Lisbon would be able to raise an expeditionary field division deployed from Angola to reinforce the Portuguese army in Europe.

The majority of these units were light infantry battalions and independent companies designated *caçadores*. These were designed to operate autonomously and, if necessary, in total isolation without much support from higher echelons in Luanda. Also, they were deployed along the lines of a grid system (*quadrícula*) in the theatre of operations, each one responsible for a given area or sector.

Usually, a regiment-sized *agrupamento* (battle group) commanded a sector, divided into several sub-sectors, each constituting an area of responsibility of a *caçadores* battalion. In turn, each battalion had its field companies dispersed and apportioned into sub-sector responsibility. From 1962, four intervention zones—Northern, Central, Southern and Eastern—were established. Renamed 'military zones' in 1967, each grouping covered a number of sectors.

Due to the low-scale guerrilla nature of the conflict, the *caçadores* or company became the main tactical unit, with the standard organization of four platoons—three rifle and one support—being replaced by one based on four identical sub-units known as 'combat groups'. Army forces also included regular units of artillery, armoured reconnaissance, engineering, communications, signal intelligence, military police and logistics. Besides regular units, it also fielded units of Special Forces, with these initially consisting of companies of special *caçadores* trained in guerrilla and counterinsurgency warfare.

Troops, clearly unconcerned about ambush, follow a river line on patrol; to some it all appears a bit of a jaunt. (Revista Militar)

The civilian administration of Angola's people (of all races) had been an important aspect of government control. Without a strong internal authority that could keep domestic issues satisfactorily ticking over, dissension would almost certainly follow, as it had scores of times during the almost five centuries that Lisbon nurtured its African colonies. Things changed radically after the invasion. In 1961 the local administration of Angola included more than a dozen districts, each with a governor at its head, assisted by a district board, working, as required, in relation to the threat level in close collaboration with the security forces. This could be the army, law enforcement elements or PIDE, the International and State Defence Police—the ultimate security establishment that was answerable to nobody but its own.

The role of Angola's black people, of absolute necessity, was considered to be of paramount importance, if only to avoid disaffection and possible linkage to guerrilla cadres. By the time hostilities started, local African auxiliary police officers, known as *cipaios*, had been instituted and these fell under what were known as administrative circles (*circunscrições*) and posts (*postos*), as in *chefe do posto*. In these regions, the traditional authorities—including native kings, rulers and tribal chiefs—were maintained intact as they had almost always been. These authorities were integrated into the administrative system and served as intermediaries between provincial authorities and the local native populations. It seemed to work quite well outside the conflict areas but once the MPLA or rival guerrilla groups like UNITA became active in a particular region, the black leaders would bow to the new authority. If they did not, they knew exactly what would happen. They would simply disappear into the night and 'friendlier faces' put in their place, as is the way with all revolutions.

4. THE ENEMY: DIVERGENT OPTIONS

As the war progressed, the three principle guerrilla adversaries spent almost as much time fighting each other as they did the Portuguese, a problem of so many insurgencies where there are multiple aspirants for power and, obviously, the money that goes with it all. In this regard, Angola was no different. Those who led the uprising were a diverse lot, some brilliant, others clearly lacking in the kind of command skills required of a leader. At the same time, every one of them was vehemently dedicated to ousting Portugal from their African homelands.

For a long time, the revolutionary whip hand in Angola was jointly held by Holden Roberto's UPA (Patriotic Union of Angola) and the MPLA, run from very early on by an academic and poet by the name of Agostinho Neto. The UPA was eventually to transmogrify into GRAE, and finally into FNLA.

Of them all, Dr Agostinho Neto, a charming young intellectual who nursed the movement through its most difficult years, was far and away the most competent. Though a revolutionary through and through, he was certainly no despot, though he could be cruel toward those who crossed him. Neto was a man regarded even by his enemies as ahead of his time and there are many party stalwarts in Luanda today who maintain that he was murdered by the Soviets while being treated at a Moscow clinic, in part because he had begun to show a predilection for possibly drawing closer to the West. Angola's first president seemed to have grown weary of Moscow's insistence on putting the party ahead of the individual. Shortly afterwards—and here we are talking about the 'middle years' of the revolution—the mid-1970s—he was heard to say that after years of fighting and untold numbers of deaths, the guerrilla struggle was going nowhere. The Portuguese, as we are now aware, were of a similar mind and had already put out feelers for some kind of political settlement.

In spite of initial misgivings, it was the MPLA, with enough Moscow-led coercion and Third World subterfuge to do justice to any communist revolutionary group, that eventually wormed its way into a position to take over the government of Angola even before the Portuguese had left for home. Curiously, the movement was assisted by the most senior Portuguese office holder in Angola, Admiral Rosa Coutinho. There is adequate evidence out there today to prove that this admiral had been a communist for many years and though he played a prominent role in Angola's war against the insurgency, nobody was in any doubt where his true allegiances lay. Yet the three main revolutionary parties were not the only players during that critical pre-independent phase. There were numerous splinter groups and offshoots with such

A large group of civilians is addressed by one of the revolutionary leaders.

illustrious titles as CPA-CNE, FLEC, FLJKP and UNITA, the last, Dr Jonas Savimbi's UNITA, arguably the most successful African guerrilla group of the 20th century, though evidence has recently surfaced that his mind went in the end.

During the Portuguese epoch in Africa, all these freedom movements operated from neighbouring states and were headquartered either in Kinshasa, Brazzaville or in the Zambian capital, Lusaka. Groups opposed to the Portuguese presence in the oil-rich Cabinda enclave, chose Brazzaville.

The UPA, or later, the National Front for the Liberation of Angola (FNLA), achieved prominence after the first bunch of revolutionaries had crossed into Angola from the Congo and started to murder and plunder. Curiously, there were some Americans intelligence operatives who believed that for all that, UPA might have been success-fully moulded into a rather promising guerrilla group, but it was not to be. Headed by Holden Roberto, the man who engineered the first full-scale attacks in March 1961, much of the support given to UPA/ FNLA came from Western-orientated countries as well as pro-African movements in the United States, Britain, France and Belgium. Other coun-tries that assisted financially and militarily were Tunisia, Ethiopia, Israel, the United Arab Republic (the short-lived union between Egypt and Syria) and, in the final stages, India.

Founded in 1954 as an illegal independence party within Angola, UPA was largely tribal-orientated. Its power rested with the half a million Bakongo people of northern

Angola, the same people who had originally welcomed early settlers from Lisbon to their shores five centuries before. And while other tribes were involved, almost all senior party positions were delegated by Roberto, who we now also know enjoyed the support of clandestine CIA-funded groups, including dissident Cubans based in Miami, Florida.*

A number of these Cuban expatriates—many of them aviators—were later hired by the CIA to fly World War II-vintage aircraft for the Congolese air force against dissident rebel forces in the east of that country.

Harvard T-6s already in the Congo were replaced by larger and more versatile T-28 Trojans, of which Washington delivered more than a dozen, as well as five long-range attack B-26 bombers, three C-47 Dakotas and two small twin-engine liaison planes. All were flown by mercenaries hired for the purpose, including Cape Town's Ares Klootwyk who had been trained in the South African Air Force (SAAF), served in the Royal Air Force where he flew jet fighters and then went on to man helicopters as well as fixed-wing aircraft in both the Congo and Biafra.**

All this had taken place a few years before Holden Alvaro Roberto—alias José Gilmore, Roberto Holden, Ruy Ventura, Onofre *et al*—and also a brother-in-law of Mobutu—came on the scene. Born in 1923 near São Salvador in Angola, a town not far from the Congolese frontier, and while still an infant, Roberto's family moved to the Belgian Congo where the future insurgent leader received most of his secondary education. The family then returned to Angola. Prior to the evolution of his revolutionary interests, Roberto went back to the Belgian Congo and worked for a while in the finance department of the colonial administration in Leopoldville (now Kinshasa), Stanleyville (Kisangani) and Bukavu in the that country's Eastern Province. During this time he retained close links with family interests in the Portuguese overseas province and consequently spoke fluent Portuguese, French, fairly good English, a little Flemish as well as his native Bakonga.

This 'Freedom Army' leader admitted to several journalists who interviewed him over many years that most of his early support came from the American Committee on Africa and the Ford Foundation, largely as a result of the efforts of Eleanor Roosevelt and former United States assistant secretary of state for African affairs, Mennen 'Soapy' Williams. A curious individual, Williams led the pack with his anti-white African rhetoric. As part of the Kennedy administration he is best remembered for declaring that "what we [the United States] want for the Africans is what they want for themselves". This was reported in the press as "Africa for the Africans",

---

* Larry Devlin, *Chief of Station, Congo*. The author crossed paths in Africa from time to time and remained in contact after Devlin had retired from Langley.
** See chapter 5 in *War Stories* by Al J. Venter & Friends which details Klootwyk's three years spent flying against the rebels in the Congo.

Che Guevara when he visited the region in the early 1960s.

Daniel Chipenda led a breakaway group of FNLA rebels that eventually defected to South Africa.

with some commentators contending that Williams was totally opposed to countries like South Africa and the Rhodesia being run by whites and wanted all people of European extraction living there permanently, expelled from the continent.

It was taken for granted that Williams was a powerful protagonist of Holden Roberto, despite the FNLA leader crediting much of his success (as well as moral support from abroad) to Patrice Lumumba, the first black Congolese politician to make any kind of impact internationally. Notably, both Roberto and Lumumba were on first-name terms with Ghanaian Kwame Nkrumah, another maverick politician who referred to himself as *Osajyefo* (Redeemer). Roberto had worked in Accra for a while from 1958 onward.

These links went deep. Roberto always maintained that "my beloved Patrice" remained his "guiding light" until Lumumba was murdered by the CIA because Washington feared his close links with the Kremlin might get out of hand. The largest 'black' educational institution in the former Soviet Union, Friendship University in Moscow, was renamed Patrice Lumumba University, after his death, a long-standing tribute to the man.

Above all, it was Washington that gave UPA/ FNLA the impetus it needed to get its revolution into some kind of functioning mode. One Belgian diplomat I met in Kinshasa a few years after the first attacks took place maintained that were it not for CIA money, the movement would have floundered at birth, or shortly afterward. It was his view that the United States fostered the UPA image as an effective counter to the more radical Congo-Brazza and Lusaka-based opposition.

It was obviously all Cold War stuff because from very early on, the MPLA enjoyed strong Soviet support: you got nowhere within that revolutionary movement if you were not a party *tovarisch*.

After more than seven years of fighting, Roberto's party took the first of many serious knocks in July 1968 when an Organization of African Unity resolution withdrew recognition of his Angolan government-in-exile. OAU (African Union today) leaders declared in Addis Ababa that they would channel all future military and financial assistance to the MPLA, already in strong opposition to UPA/ FNLA. The reason for the choice, the media was told, was that the MPLA appeared to be the more successful fighting group in Angola.

Veteran guerrilla fighter and Cuban protégé, Henrique 'Iko' Carreira became independent Angola's first defence minister.

Indirectly, Lisbon concurred that this was a logical choice. By the time I arrived in Luanda for the first time in the mid-1960s—I was on my way to London—the Portuguese military authorities were candid that the MPLA threat was the most serious they had encountered since the start of the war. In fact, they made no bones about it: the MPLA and the Conakry-based PAIGC movement operating in Portuguese Guinea were the most effective guerrilla armies in sub-Saharan Africa, which became the most significant theme of my first briefing.

It was the same with training. MPLA cadres were put through their paces by just about every communist country on the planet. It even included involving North Vietnamese guerrilla veterans who were seconded operationally to Angola in the later stages of the liberation war. These military specialists from South East Asia were put to good use in breaking the language barrier, especially since many rebel volunteers had originally come from Francophone Africa. Because that part of South East Asia—Indo-China it was called—had formerly been a French colony, it made good sense.

Dr Agostinho Neto, in direct contrast to Holden Roberto, apart from being what his biographers called—"a quiet spoken intellectual and poet"—was also a Portuguese national, only he completed his tertiary studies in Lisbon. For a while in the early days, Neto operated from an office in central Lusaka, though his movement's military wing—in large part because of CIA involvement in the region—had previously been based in Congo-Brazzaville but increased French influence later forced him southward.

Ultimately the Zambian government's militant stand against newly independent Rhodesia was the deciding factor in Portuguese liberation groups gaining Kenneth Kaunda's support. The country's geographical position between three of the four erstwhile European-dominated southern African states made the former British colony an excellent staging post.

Throughout the liberation struggle, Neto maintained a host of representatives in Europe—both East and West—as well as in Peking, Havana, Cairo, Lagos, Conakry and Algiers. In some they were afforded full diplomatic status. His links with FRELIMO, the Mozambican insurgent group once headed by another American favourite, the late Eduardo Mondlane, were close. Following Mondlane's murder (never solved, and still today believed to be part of an internal power struggle orchestrated by Samora Machel), Neto was said to have become more reclusive and in the minds some of his lieutenants, even isolated from the party. He feared, correctly, that he might be next.

In contrast, Daniel Chipenda, who had once been a senior MPLA office bearer, was a competent but testy revolutionary and might even had become head of this radical movement had ambition not prompted him to move on. Though he later fell out with some of the elders of the founding party, he was initially the MPLA representative in Dar es Salaam, where his job was to coordinate training and supply programmes with other liberation groups in southern Africa. It was an important posting because a large proportion of the military hardware used by the MPLA—as well as Mozambican and Rhodesian liberation groups—was channelled through

March past of
guerrilla cadres in
northern Angola.

MPLA recruit
training in
the Congo.

Dar es Salaam harbour. Chipenda must have used his position to good personal effect which would obviously have been linked to money, since it was said he was working for both the CIA and South African Military Intelligence. This was why it came no surprise when he formed his own political and military grouping that he called the Chipa Squadron, or in the lingo, *Chipa Esquadrão*. It was this band of fairly seasoned fighters that went over to the South African army almost *en bloc*

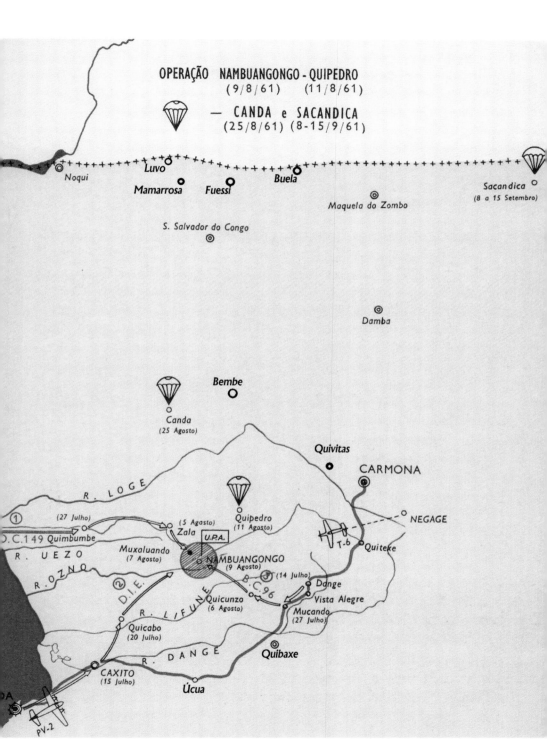

The Portuguese reoccupation of the north of Angola.

Following a landmine incident, a Portuguese soldier approaches an Alouette while on convoy duty.

A Soviet TB-46 anti-tank mine uncovered by a sapper along a bush road.

A patrol emerges from the jungle into marshland.

FNLA troops being put
through their paces,
on a 12.7mm heavy
machine gun.

For much of the year,
roads in the north were
impassable because of
tropical rains.

A Harvard armed with
rockets does a pass over
a prospective target
in the north.

Harvards
returning to base
after an airstrike.

Nambuagongo
was briefly
the rebel
headquarters in
northern Angola.

Troops emplane to
a Puma helicopter.

Panhards at a
Luanda national
day parade.

A Portuguese Air
Force F-86 Sabre at
Luanda airport.

A Harvard sortie.

Bombing up Portuguese
Air Force F-84s at Luanda.

Left: Portuguese troops
deployed in northern
Angola earlier on were not
well organized.

Below: Portuguese Air
Force Nord Noratlas
freighter.

A Portuguese army truck destroyed by a landmine.

Right: Portuguese operations in the east of the country.

Below: Army convoy.

A Puma helicopter uplifting an army patrol in open savannah.

Army conscripts torch a civilian hut, suspected of harbouring the enemy.

A Harvard over the lush Angolan terrain.

Counterinsurgency operations in southeastern Angola.

after the Portuguese had pulled out. The unit was eventually shaped into the SADF's crack 32 Battalion Special Forces group by Jan Breytenbach.[*]

Gradually the MPLA proved to be the more forceful of the two liberation groups, largely because Neto was receiving arms, equipment and training from the Kremlin that outmatched anything the Americans had on offer. Also, his movement by then had quietly taken in scores of experienced fighters from other conflicts who had answered the call, including a number of Cuban militants.

Meanwhile, the CIA had recruited Holden Roberto who was found to be both inept and ineffectual in command and it is curious that he was never replaced, or possibly his brother-in-law Mobutu Sese Seko had something to do with that.

At Moscow's behest, Castro had been consistently following developments and Cuba entered the fray in force shortly afterwards. Neto had already met Che Guevara and soon got an infusion of cash from Havana as well as from East Germany.

In May 1966, Daniel Chipenda—then still a member of the MPLA—established the Eastern Front, significantly expanding the group's reach. But when that effort collapsed, Chipenda and Neto blamed each other for what has since been described as a tactical blunder that should never have happened. However, it did and one of the results was that Luanda strengthened both its command structure and its forces in the east though even this eventually produced little of substance.

During the late 1960s the FNLA and MPLA ended up spending a lot of effort and lives at each other's throats. It got so bad that MPLA forces eventually assisted Lisbon's PIDE security agents in hunting down FNLA hideouts.

A brief word about Agostinho Neto the man

Born in September 1922 at Icolo e Bengo, south of Nova Lisboa in Angola's central provinces, he was educated to secondary level at a Luanda school. From 1944 to 1947 he worked in the Portuguese health services in the city and it was then that his zeal and initiative prompted the authorities to allow him to study medicine at Coimbra University in Portugal.

Not much was known about his politics at this stage, but one of his associates labelled him a 'visionary' because young Neto believed that eventually black people would rule his land. What is clear is that, studies or not, Agostinho Neto became

---

[*] During the final phase of the Portuguese withdrawal from Angola, the author travelled from Luanda to Nova Lisboa (since renamed Huambo) to join Daniel Chipenda's *Chipa Esquadrão* as a mercenary, largely in order to get the story he was after. The relationship did not last long. South African army units had meanwhile invaded northward from South West Africa (today's Namibia) and had made inroads almost as far north as Luanda. Obviously, his presence as a South African journalist impeded progress since the entire operation was supposed to be covert.

MPLA leader Agostinho Neto with his mentor, Fidel Castro.

politically active and five years later, in 1952, was imprisoned for taking part in popular demonstrations against his hosts.

Although freed shortly afterward, he was imprisoned again from February 1955 for almost thirty months. Neto qualified as a doctor in 1958 and the same day he was awarded his diploma in Lisbon he married his Portuguese wife.

Dr Neto's MPLA was originally established in Luanda in 1956 as an underground movement advocating equal rights for all people irrespective of race, colour or creed. Prior to its exile to Congo-Brazza, the MPLA merged with a number of political groupings declared illegal by the Portuguese authorities. From early on, Neto was assisted by other radical members, including his close associate Mário Pinto de Andrade who lived outside Africa for most of his life. During the course of his studies in Lisbon, Frankfurt and Paris, Andrade joined both the Portuguese (underground) and French communist parties and spent time doing what his biographers term 'political training' in Moscow, Warsaw and Peking.

The date the MPLA commemorates above all others is 4 February: it features in the name of Luanda's international airport. Then, in 1961—almost six weeks before the first UPA attacks had taken place in northern Angola—MPLA guerrillas attacked the São Paulo prison. Neto always maintained that the large-scale UPA/ GRAE attacks were

Female MPLA troops played a valuable role in the war.

premature. Had Roberto waited a few months, he reckoned, their joint efforts would have had a far more devastating effect on the Portuguese security forces. Luanda might even have fallen, he wrote afterwards and he was probably right because, following the first rebel attacks, Lisbon's defenders were forced the fall back almost to the city gates.

The MPLA also liked to claim responsibility for opening Angola's 'Second Front' in the east, along the Zambian border, an area of infiltration that the Portuguese military authorities in Luanda admitted in their briefings was already larger than Rhodesia's by the late 1960s. For a long time, most of the preliminary training that MPLA and UPA/ GRAE/ FNLA recruits underwent was completed in Zambia, Zaire, Congo-Brazza and Tanzania. A number of insurgent training camps were pinpointed early on in various African states bordering southern Africa, including Doliesie and Pointe Noire in Congo-Brazza; Kinkuzu, which was a large UPA/ FNLA camp some miles south of Kinshasa in Zaire/ Congo; Tanzania's Kongwa, Bagamoyo and Nachingwea towns as well as Sikongo in the Barotse Province of Zambia.

Many of the brighter young MPLA trainees were sent for advanced guerrilla instruction at military institutions farther afield. The huge guerrilla training base at Tclemen, Algeria, regarded by many as the ultimate in revolutionary training orientation in Africa, was rated by the West as a terrorist-style 'African West Point' and quite a few recruits loyal to Neto spent a good deal of time there. The same with Muammar Gadaffi's revolutionary headquarters at Sabha, deep in the Sahara Desert, about

A canny guerrilla leader, UNITA leader Jonas Savimbi gave Lisbon many headaches.

800 kilometres south of Tripoli. American mercenary aviator Dana Drenkowski—he flew 200 combat missions in Vietnam in B-52s and Phantoms—ended up there after he had been hired by the Libyan strongman and was astonished by the number of radicals he encountered there, the IRA especially.[*]

Portuguese military leaders maintained throughout the Angolan colonial phase of the war that a major factor in favour of their own forces in the struggle was that UPA and MPLA—while opposed to Portuguese domination—went to war with one another as soon as they did. Of the two, MPLA guerrillas were by far the most resilient: better trained, tough, wily and totally ruthless, as former PIDE operative Oscar Cardozo phrased it when I spent a bit of time with him after he had fetched me from N'Requinha in Angola's far east. General Bettencourt Rodrigues—the man who had originally arranged for me to cover these wars—once commented that "many MPLA cadres have been well trained ... they know what they want and they know how to get it." He knew what he was talking about. I stayed in touch with him over the years and it was clear to anybody who knew the man that he was an outstanding field commander. It was Bettencourt Rodrigues who pulled Lisbon's troops up by their bootstraps when he was finally posted to senior command in Angola.

The UPA/ FNLA, in contrast, was soon weakened by a lack of discipline that seemed to dog its efforts all the way up the ladder to headquarters in Kinshasa. Holden Roberto ruled largely by decree and preferred the good life—and all the hooch that went with it—in the Congolese capital, especially since it was subsidised by Langley. He ended up a chronic alcoholic and, to the surprise of us all, was one of the few of the old guard who actually died in his own bed, of heart disease in 2007.

There were other notable differences between the two guerrilla factions. Whereas MPLA guerrillas would *ask* villagers for food and normally pay for what they took, UPA fighters would demand it as their right and make no recompense. For Neto's guerrillas, it was one of the simple revolutionary principles picked up in Mao's China. More salient, MPLA cadres were always very correct in their dealings with the locals

---

[*]   Dana Drenkowski's adventures while working with the Libyans—which almost got him killed—is detailed in chapter 9 of the author's *War Dog: Fighting Other People's Wars*.

they encountered while on operations in the bush. That was something apparently drummed into them while they were in training. UPA men, in contrast, just took what they wanted, often at gunpoint. In one area, an officer told me, a UPA officer had shot a tribal chief because he had objected to his men taking three young virgins of the village for their pleasure. "That would never have been tolerated in any area controlled by the MPLA," he said. The philosophy behind its strategy was basic and involved a simple maxim: 'Help us now and once in power, you will not be forgotten.' This was where the Chinese and Cuban influences immediately become apparent, Sector D's Brigadier Martins

Typical rebel patrol in Portuguese Africa. Note the RPG-2s in the column.

Soares maintained at one of his briefings. MPLA units, he stated, were implementing the Chinese communist dogma: before it was possible to win a guerrilla struggle it was necessary to win the confidence of the civilian population. "They must move as freely among the civilians as the fishes in the sea," the Chinese revolutionary leader wrote, an aphorism that became engrained in many subsequent revolutionary struggles on several continents. The MPLA enshrined it.

Perhaps the best illustration of MPLA efficacy and where they made headway, the brigadier said, was that when their young men returned to an area after being trained abroad they spent time organizing the villagers to tidy their living quarters and make more equable sanitary arrangements. It was healthier for the entire community, they would explain. They would then encourage young men of the villages to help their women grow more crops, something unheard of in stratified tribal circles where it had always been females responsible for tending to the needs of the family.

Applying simple administrative principles was usually enough to impress any village chief who had lived in the jungle most of his life. In any event, to these simple African folk, enthusiastic young MPLA guerrillas were more reliable than either the usually obnoxious Portuguese government functionaries with whom all had had fleeting contact, or their grab-all UPA adversaries.

5. JOURNALISTS

Angola in wartime was a rather different place when compared to other cities caught up in an unpredictable vortex of violence. It was not at all like Saigon while that South East Asian conflict raged and bore no resemblance whatever to what was going on in Beirut shortly afterwards. Arriving in Luanda on my four-month, largely overland journey from Johannesburg to London toward the end of 1965 was a revelation. I'd been there before, while a crewmember serving on board a naval frigate, but that was 1959 and the war was still two years away. Also, we were showing the flag as it were, with everything quite formal: honour guards, parades, diplomatic functions and the rest.

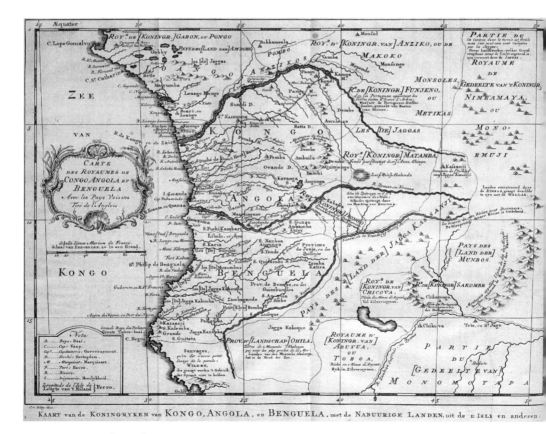

A 1747 map of Angola.

The second time round, already four years into the colonial war, was very different. I discovered in Luanda a boisterous, bustling city that was unlike any other place I'd ever visited. The Angolan capital had achieved a remarkable reputation as one of the out-of-the-way treasures of the Third World. It had actually been dubbed by several visiting scribes as an African version of Rio. One called it Portugal's 'New Horizon'.

I found in Luanda an affluent, breezily insouciant modern city, coupled to a thoroughly cosmopolitan and multiracial society. Its waterfront, centre-city area buzzed from before dawn until very late at night. I would have my morning *café-com-leite* and bread rolls in a large workers' kind of transport cafe with enormous wooden windows near the dockside and it cost me the equivalent of about a dollar. Luanda's suburbs were a lot like Cape Town today: prosperous, millionaire-style suburbs only a rifle-shot from mind-blowing poverty in slums that were both execrable and dangerous.

The city boasted a range of excellent schools and the biggest Portuguese-language university in Africa, with almost as many faculties as the University of Cape Town and with many more black students than I expected. The city even boasted a privately owned observatory on the one of the hills overlooking the Marginal, as the road adjacent to the harbour was called. Beyond that were the beaches and the restaurants and though exceptionally low cost, they were world class. You could get a meal of curried prawns or chicken peri-peri and a carafe of wine for what you would pay for a cup of coffee in a London Starbucks today. A taxi ride into town was about the same, all in Angolan escudos, linked in those days to Lisbon's Banco de Portugal.

One of Africa's oldest forts, the one at Luanda, seen here from the bay.

And while men in uniform were hardly a rarity in the restaurants and clubs, this did not seem like a nation battling to cope with an extremely demanding war. Part of the reason, of course, could have been that the average Portuguese conscript was paid a pittance compared to his European counterparts and simply could not afford any of these fancy places. I stayed in Luanda on that visit for almost two weeks and it was a charm. It was not long before I'd joined a small group of student friends and after hours we'd move about the city from one night spot to another. In the process I discovered a vital, dynamic conurbation, the likes of which I had never dreamed possible north of the Zambezi.

The city was well ordered and while the majority of blacks were poor, they seemed to keep their spirits alive by decorating or cleaning their front and back yards and sometimes even mended potholes in their streets.

There were actually several comparisons with South Africa. The European settler community in Angola was forthright and uncompromising in its views, whether about food, entertainment, politics or sport. This was also a much healthier outdoor community than that of their relatives in the *metrópole*.

Army instructors in Lisbon would often complain that new conscripts who arrived for their basic military training in Europe were often below par physically, but that was rare in Angola. In this African colony people were accustomed to lengthy sporting

Cannon line the ramparts of the old fort in Luanda.

sessions at school or perhaps heading out into the bush with their families or fishing down the coast, for no other reason than that they liked doing so. In Luanda, Lobito and Nova Lisboa—which, after independence was to change its name to Huambo—the emphasis among the youth was on education, sport and culture in roughly that order of priority: just about every youngster whose parents could afford it aspired to a university degree

Things came fairly easy in Angola in those days because prices had not been bumped up by tourists: there were hardly any. Portugal was coping with its conflicts but anybody who wished to visit the country would have had to have a very good reason for doing so before they could gain entry. That category obviously excluded American and European hunting fraternities: Angola boasted some the best wildlife safaris on the continent. But, as the saying goes, that was all strictly 'big bucks'.

Replica of one of the crosses left on the African coast by Lisbon's early mariners. (Caroline Castell)

Like today, the city was divided into two parts, the Baixa de Luanda (lower Luanda, the old city) and the Cidade Alta (upper city or the new part). With its narrow streets and old colonial buildings, the Baixa was situated next to the port, and it was there that my friends and I would spend most of our evenings. And, if the mood took me, I could get a day job on one of the boats that plied the coast and accept my wages in fish once we got back to port, which would provide me and my student friends with dinner: Angola was that kind of place in the old days.

It was an idyllic life, and I would have liked to stay. But the rest of Africa beckoned, and at the end of it, I had to get to London.

Quite a few other journalists shared these views and one of them was John Miller who was assigned to Cape Town as southern African correspondent for the *Daily Telegraph*. He was as enthusiastic about Luanda as I was and only managed the elusive visa because his newspaper, though not emphatically pro-Portuguese, was a lot more positive about white people in Africa than most other British broadsheets, as it was too with Rhodesians when their troubles began.

I was doing some work on the Portuguese colonies on my return from covering the wars there and for a modest fee—which John would probably spend at the nineteenth hole of his golf club, he penned a few words on his return from a visit to the 'war front' north of Luanda.

This was his 1973 report—a year before the colonial war ended—which I quote *in toto*:

Luanda, the capital of Angola, Portugal's largest overseas territory, is a handsome city which need not fear comparison with any other city in tropical Africa. Because the Portuguese in Africa have their roots in Angola, it has a bustling business quarter and docks, an old-fashioned and curiously designed Governor-General's palace and government offices, a castle built in 1638 and still dominating the city—and São João, an old fortress, now a common prison.

On 4 February 1961 around the grim walls of São João were fired the first shots in a war which has plagued Portugal ever since. In a swift surprise attack under cover of darkness, a group of Africans armed with machetes and shotguns attacked the prison. It is just another of the many ironies of revolutionary history that the group had hoped to free political prisoners but there were none there at the time. In any event, a handful of prison guards drove the attackers back to the opulent Miramar residential district, where the richest of the descendants of the early Portuguese colonizers, civil servants and products of recent immigration cowered in their homes clutching pistols and sporting rifles.

During a long and confusing night the Africans regrouped and struck at the police headquarters. It was here that revolutionary first blood was shed. Eight policemen and thirty-six of the attackers were killed and sixty-three other Europeans and Africans wounded. Many more were to die the next day, when, at a series of funeral processions, some white nationals who demanded reprisals went on the rampage.

The death toll during the two days was insignificant compared to what was to follow later that year—and every year since. African nationalism had tasted blood in Angola, over which Portugal's red and green flag had fluttered for nearly 500 years, and there was no going back. Inevitably a lull in the fighting was followed by a storm.

Then came the invasion and Lisbon and Dr Antonio Salazar, the man of granite, were powerless to halt the wave of bloodshed, for there were no Portuguese soldiers in Carmona Province, which is the size of Portugal itself, and as few as 3,000 troops in two regiments in the whole of Angola. Not surprisingly, considering the ferocity and determination of the freedom fighters, the massacre continued for a fortnight. If it was not the biggest slaughter of whites which has taken place in Africa in this century, it was not far short of it. What is certain is that it passed almost unnoticed in the world press.

By the end of 1961, thousands of Portuguese troops rushed from Lisbon were beginning to get to grips with the situation. The freedom fighters still attacked farms and villages and laid ambushes from impenetrable bush, but the spark had not led to a roaring inferno. What had happened was that some 2,000 Whites and an estimated 50,000 Africans had been killed. War had come to Angola, where the Portuguese had dozed for centuries and the long and lazy colonial siesta was over. The year 1961 marked the beginning of what has since become a continual challenge to the Portuguese to stay in Africa.

For twelve wearisome years the Portuguese, and those of mixed European and African descent, as well as the six million Africans, have been learning to live with their grim little war. And there are ever-present reminders of it. On every street in every town and village there were soldiers, white and black, swaggering and conspicuous in their jungle camouflage uniforms. The original 3,000 had become 60,000.

In Carmona Province each and every *fazenda* was surrounded by barbed wire, and day and night armed sentries stood in the obligatory high white towers. In the railway workshops of Nova Lisboa in the heart of the country workers fitted armour plate to pilot trucks travelling the long line to the east, or they patched up sabotaged engines. Across the country the walled and guarded military posts bristling with radio masts were always on the alert, their heavy machine-guns well-oiled and swivelling free.

And in Luanda on a Saturday afternoon, a slice on the 17th tee of the local golf course could mean trouble if the ball could hit a descending paratrooper. As it was, golfers played to the background of crackling small-arms fire from the nearby military range and the constantly rising and falling snarl of army helicopters.

Overhead American Harvard trainer/ground-support aircraft of World War II vintage simulated bomb and napalm attacks and the immensely useful French-built Noratlas troop carriers lumbered in, bringing the dead and the maimed, or simply tired young conscripts aching for the bright lights, bars and brothels of a Western-style city. And often Luanda golfers have to hold back their drives for fear of hitting the halftracks and trucks crammed with troops that are ceaselessly rattling along the road cutting through the back nine holes, and going God knows where.

But Luanda was 'safe'. It had not heard a shot fired since those dark days of 1961. The terse little communiqués of actions and ambushes, of who killed whom, how and where, hardly ever made front-page news in Luanda newspapers, and in any case, as in Vietnam at its worst, were seldom read.

The reality of a protracted anti-guerrilla war came home to you however on the convoy run from 'safe' Luanda to Carmona farther north where hostilities were an everyday thing.

There were two roads to Carmona. One swept south-east from Luanda to Salazar and then north. It was the best part of a day's drive and it was said to be safe from ambush. The other road, which struck straight north, was shorter, more direct—and dangerous.

The danger zone rolled north from Cuixita, an hour's drive from Luanda. Here swarthy Portuguese truck drivers came face to face with the reality of a guerrilla war, with the fact they could just possibly die from a sniper's bullet, or a Russian or Chinese landmine lovingly laid in a lousy road. But the job had to be done. And every day for several years, heavy trucks taking food and supplies to hamlets along the route had to be marshalled, counted and protected.

The convoy run to Carmona began at seven in the morning and the 350-kilometre drive took all of thirteen hours. When I joined it, a bearded African corporal was listing the truck numbers and pulling the convoy into line.

Soon the lead army vehicle with a mounted and shielded heavy machine gun and eight soldiers with their Heckler & Koch G3 automatic rifles eased away

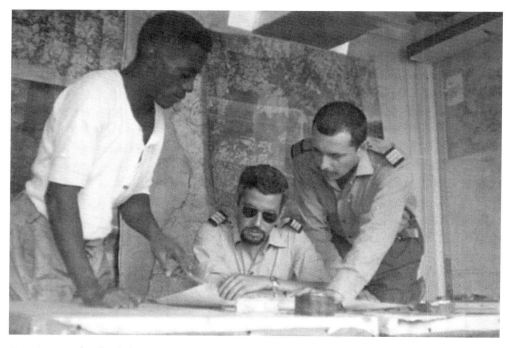

Captain Ricardo Alcada (centre) who accompanied the author in Angola's north.

from the local bar where the soldiers had been having bad Portuguese brandy and better coffee and took up point position. Another similarly equipped vehicle roared and rattled down from the local military base to cover the convoy's rear.

For the first hour's ride to Ucua over a twisting, atrociously bad road, the truck drivers fought to get behind the lead army vehicle. Horns blared as the trucks jumped the potholes and swayed from side to side. It was not fear so much as the one-hour stop at a hamlet with two bars, half a dozen stray dogs, the army and a house of camp-followers which drove them on.

There the game ended, for the next 170 kilometres to Carmona was deadly serious business. The sergeant with the machine-gunner's eyes swept the towering bush grass, jungle and hills while the rest of the platoon nervously fingered their weapons. Not far from the surface of the jaunt through classic guerrilla warfare country was the knowledge that someone could get killed if anyone were careless.

The convoy hugged itself through to Checkpoint Three. There it waited for another convoy—this one bound for Luanda—to be cleared by a slip of a lad with a bundle of grenades at his feet and a clipboard in his hand.

To kill time and escape from the heat of the fierce midday sun, the truck drivers slipped away up the hill to the Portuguese army 'farm', complete with a mini soccer pitch, and bristling with heavy machine-guns and updated bazookas. For an hour or two we drank beer with the three platoons who sat it out on the hill month after month with nothing to pass the time but a pack of cards, a battery-driven portable record player and the African women who sat passively on the grimy army camp beds.

This was what the war in Angola is largely all about: sitting it out, waiting for an attack which rarely came. This was what the Portuguese called 'terrorist-infected country'. It probably was. But because the freedom fighters could only hit the convoys or the military 'farms' at their peril, it could fairly be said that the Portuguese had managed to contain the war in Angola.

They controlled the densely populated, economically viable areas of a territory nearly half the size of Western Europe. They were keeping the guerrilla movements at bay in the useless under-populated areas, and they were pushing through as rapidly as possible—for Portuguese bureaucracy had been a deadening hand in the past—the economic, social, cultural and medical reforms necessary for a counter-revolution against African nationalism.

6. THE AIR WAR

It was clear from the very beginning of the Angolan war that the Portuguese would have to fight very differently to what other nations had been doing. For a start, it was the era of the helicopter gunship, but Lisbon was never able to afford the luxury of unlimited air assets like the Americans enjoyed in Vietnam.

It was air power that eventually turned the war around for Portugal: literally from a no-hope situation to a credible advance that continued to take giant steps as hostilities continued. Following the 1952 reorganization of the Portuguese air force from the army and naval air arms, Lisbon's armed forces emerged with an entity dedicated solely to aviation that would bring it into line with its new NATO commitment. The problem, as Portugal was to discover less than a decade later, was that it was hardly geared for counterinsurgency efforts under primitive African conditions. As the Portuguese air force proceeded to develop a competence in modern multi-engine and jet fighter aircraft for its NATO role and train a professional corps of pilots, it was suddenly confronted in 1961 with the invasion of Angola from the Congo. This development forced it to acquire an entirely new and separate air force, appropriately, but not officially called the African Air Force to address this emerging danger.

The aircraft available at the time were nothing as sophisticated as so many of its NATO partners were flying and the majority of those already in Angola were hardly suited for counterinsurgency roles. To the surprise of all, because Portugal had always been slow to act in the past, it briskly adapted them to the task and effectively crafted the appropriate strategies and tactics for their successful employment.

Mainly due to an international arms embargo to which Portugal was subjected, its air force had to struggle with limited funds and access to new machines. That meant extending the operational use of many out-of-date aircraft. As an example, in its bid to cover all Angolan regions in which there had been hostilities in 1972, plus ancillary non-combatant regions—a territory twice the size of Spain—the FAP had available something like thirty helicopters, forty-four light aircraft, thirteen transport planes, six light bombers and a squadron or two of jet fighters regarded by most as well past the age of retirement.

After two Portuguese air force jets were brought down by Strela SAM-7 missiles in Guinea, the entire airstrike force was threatened with grounding. By implementing protective measures, the air force was able to quickly fully resume operations, adopting mitigating measures that included changing flight profiles as well as painting the planes with reflective anti-radiation paint.

Harvard aircrews back
at base after a sortie.

As Captain Jack Cann—himself a highly experienced naval aviator in the US Marines—tells us in his book *Flight Plan Africa*, the vicissitudes of procurement, an exercise fraught with anti-colonial political undercurrents, the imaginative modification and adaptation of the aircraft to fight in the African theatres, as well as the development of tactics, techniques, and procedures for their effective employment against an elusive, clever, and dangerous enemy all came into play, usually concurrently.

Unquestionably, Portuguese airpower was the critical component in their counter-insurgency campaigns and the air force responded well to the challenge despite its limited and obsolescent equipment, much of which performed well in a very hostile environment. Even today, there is value to be gained in studying how the Portuguese went about the task and the lessons they learned.

The use of air power in Africa contrasted starkly with the air war in Vietnam. Indeed, fighting in Angola very soon became a major logistics issue, specifically centred on distances that needed to be covered. Angola and Mozambique were spread about vast areas and included a great variety of terrain, from desert to jungle to savannah that stretched from one horizon to another for hundreds of kilometres at a stretch. Only with aviation was it possible to cover these areas.

From 1961 to 1974, the Portuguese air force was deeply engaged in the three theatres of hostilities in Africa, both with aviation and paratrooper forces. In the *Ultramar*, the PAF had both strategic and tactical air missions.

The strategic mission consisted of the inter-territorial connection between European Portugal and Angola, Mozambique and the much closer Portuguese Guinea just south of Senegal, like Angola on the Atlantic coast. To start with DC-6s were extensively used and, later, Boeing 707s. After acquiring the passenger jets in the early 1970s, the air force was able take a much larger share of the transport missions that until then were handled by merchant ships, reducing the connection time between the different territories from something like weeks to hours.

The tactical missions undertaken by the Portuguese air force in all three theatres were:

- Attack missions in Angola—independent, reconnaissance, support and escort—involved F-86 and F-84 fighters, PV-2 Harpoons and B-26 Invader bombers as well as Texan T-6 Harvard light attack aircraft, the latter three all World War II vintage. Earlier on France sold Alouette helicopters that were used in a gunship role, followed a decade later by Aerospatiale Pumas. Dornier Do-27 light aircraft armed with rockets were flown in some of these missions.
- Reconnaissance missions—visual and photo—using light aircraft like the PGMA/ Auster D-5 became a regular feature of the war, as did P-2 Neptunes, C-47 Dakotas and other aircraft prepared for air photo-reconnaissance;
- Tactical transportation missions—assault, manoeuvre, general and casualty evacuation (casevac)—used the full range of French helicopters.
- Transport throughout Angola was handled by the ubiquitous Nord Noratlas, which was to be seen at all regular airports in the country, as was the C-47.
- Other missions—liaison, control, operational air command post, VIP transportation and others—involved several types of aircraft.

The missions were generally carried away from a well-developed network of airbases and other airfields. By the early 1970s, in the Angolan theatre there was a central airbase, two sector airbases, eight satellite airfields and nine other airfields. In the Guinean theatre there was a central airbase, three satellite airfields and other three airfields.

In Angola—as with Mozambique—Volunteer Air Formation (FAV, *Formações Aéreas Voluntárias*) units were formed, composed of civilian volunteer pilots who assisted the air force in several missions, mostly transport and reconnaissance, using both civilian and military light aircraft.

The PAF also participated in ground and air-ground operations with its paratroopers, which became a significant factor in ongoing counterinsurgency tactics. In the early days, these troops went into action by parachute, but were later mainly deployed in air-assault operations involving Alouette and Puma helicopters.

Besides the four regular paratrooper battalions—one in Angola, one in Portuguese Guinea and two in Mozambique—the air force was also involved in the creation of the elite Paratrooper Special Groups.

In order to terminate the guerrilla infiltrations across Angola's northern border, a special composite aviation/ paratrooper unit—integrating trackers, paratroopers,

Above: Alouette gunship hovers over a landmine incident in eastern Angola.

Right: An Alouette touches down in heavy bush.

helicopters and light aircraft—was created, becoming the Counter Infiltration Tactical Unit (*Unidade Táctica de Contra-Infiltração*).

Advances in weaponry, such as with helicopter gunship, were the outgrowth of Portugal's combat needs and it was those campaigns that developed the deployment of gunships into a highly developed, lethal skill. It took time to master many of the intricacies involved, but it was not long before a lone Alouette III with a single 20mm cannon (and sometimes a double) poking out its rear port door could turn an ambush or even a full-scale rumble in the jungle around, literally within minutes. In the process, Portuguese casualties were substantially limited.

The helicopter gunship concept in the PAF was built around the 20-man combat group. A flight of five Alouettes would each insert a four-man section after a target had been pinpointed, usually by ground forces. They would then hover nearby to provide covering fire if requested.

The Rhodesians, who learned from the Portuguese, also acquired a large number of these sturdy little machines that soon proved able to absorb an astonishing amount of punishment for their own bush war and refined the concept of the Fire Force, which Chris Cocks ably describes in his own book while serving in the Rhodesian Light Infantry.*

As hostilities in Angola expanded, it soon became clear to Pretoria that Lisbon's ground forces needed help: as a consequence a limited number of South African gunships were detached from the SAAF base at Ondangwa in northern South West Africa to do duty with Portuguese forces in the sandy wastes of southeast Angola. It proved invaluable experience for the South African pilots as their own 'border war' loomed large.**

Among the few specialists in this kind of Third World warfare under extremely primitive conditions, Robert Craig Johnson is among the most authoritative. Unheralded, he has provided us with many insights over the years, as he did when he explains how Portugal adapted World War II planes to good effect in her African wars.*** Like the French before them in Algeria, the Portuguese turned to outdated aircraft in their search for effective anti-guerrilla weapons. The air force had a number of Lockheed-Vega PV-2 Harpoon light patrol bombers that were tasked with anti-submarine operations along the coasts of Portugal and the Azores. They were totally obsolete and were unlikely to be missed if diverted from their official NATO role.

Certainly, the Harpoons were well suited to counterinsurgency duties. Johnson explains why:

The basic PV-2 carried five forward-firing .50-cal machine guns, two in the upper nose and three in an under-nose gun pack. The PV-2D model, of which the service had two, carried eight guns, all grouped in the lower nose. Both models could accommodate up to a ton and a half of bombs internally and up to eight five-inch HVAR rockets and napalm tanks under the wings. All defensive armament was removed to save weight.

Lisbon also noted the success of France's armed T-6 'Tomcats' in Algeria and since fighting was then winding down in that country and the elderly T-6s were being replaced, the Portuguese were able to obtain large numbers

---

   *   Chris Cocks, *Fireforce: One Man's War in the Rhodesian Light Infantry.*
  ** Al J. Venter, *Battle for Angola: The End of the Cold War in Africa c. 1975–1989.*
 ***Robert Craig Johnson, *COIN: The Portuguese in Africa, 1959–1975* (Part 2).

of fully armed, ex-*armée de l'Air* aircraft. They managed to get some Federal German Luftwaffe T-6Gs as well and modified them for combat at the central air force maintenance base outside Lisbon.

With four 7.92mm machine guns in underwing pods and 37mm Matra SNEB rocket packs, the T-6s were particularly useful for supporting infantry patrols in contacts involving small, insurgent bands and for convoy escort. But they suffered heavily during attacks on insurgent bases, where Soviet 12.7mm anti-aircraft weapons were often encountered.

Unlike the French, the Portuguese had to rely heavily on their jet fighters for COIN operations. Portugal had approximately 125 F-84G Thunderjets and sixty-five North American F-86F Sabres on hand when the rebellion began, but it could not afford to buy additional combat craft purely for use in the colonies. The F-84Gs were the first to go to Africa.

As Johnson states, this reliance on their jets placed the Portuguese in an invidious position vis-à-vis their principle ally, the United States. All these aircraft were American and all had been supplied under American military aid programmes. The United States supplied the planes on the understanding that they would be dedicated to NATO for the defence of Europe and not to quell revolutions in Africa. By diverting them for deployment in their colonies, Portugal, in American eyes, was in breach of

Alouettes airlifting casualties to hospital after a contact.

A PAF Dornier after landing at Nambuangongo following its liberation in 1962.

contract. Moreover, by doing so, they were compromising NATO security and embarrassing the United States at a time when it was trying to establish good relations with newly independent African states. The US blocked shipments of replacements and spares and kept up a barrage of protests and diplomatic pressure. By October 1964, Portugal had to withdraw the Sabres from Bissau, as Johnson tells us. The F-84s in Angola were somehow overlooked. Perhaps, having made its point over the Sabres, Washington chose to turn a blind eye, or possibly the F-84s were so manifestly obsolete that they weren't considered worth worrying about.

Thereafter the Portuguese acquired a bunch of B-26 Invaders, an aircraft that had served with distinction in Laos, Vietnam, and the nearby Congo. But by the time the Portuguese started shopping for them, they were already well past their prime. In spite of mechanical problems, a clutch of these old bombers were obtained by fair means and foul from various sources, refurbished in Tucson, Arizona and ferried to Portugal via Canada. Says Johnson: "The Portuguese air force's central maintenance facility, OGMA, then fitted armament and brought the aircraft up to military standards. The rear cockpit canopy was replaced with a metal fairing, more powerful radios were installed, and extra fuel tanks fitted in the bomb bay. Several B-26C models were converted to B-type 'strafers' at the same time."

A pilot in his F-86 awaiting takeoff at Luanda.

I flew in many Portuguese air force planes during my various visits to all three embattled war zones, but it was in Angola where most of this activity took place. That routine was apparently repeated many times each week and included largely perishables and spare parts which might take too long on the road run which was always problematic, not only because of landmines laid by the enemy, but because of bridges occasionally washed away.

Prior to acquiring six civil-version N-2502A Noratlas from one of France's regional airlines in November 1960, Lisbon was obliged to depend on its C-47 fleet, of which it had dozens. Six more Noratlases came from the Israeli air force and another three from Algeria. Over the years thirteen more were bought from the West Germans, bringing their total up to twenty-nine. Coming from so many sources the Noratlas freighters were not easy to maintain but the Portuguese army could probably not have survived without them.

Certainly the most valuable assets in Portuguese air force livery were American-built F-86G Sabres and F-84 Thunderjets. The F-86 was a formidable aircraft, with a normal armament consisting of six .50-calibre machine guns, two 1,000-pound bombs as well as four 1.75-inch rockets. The bombs might have been general purpose or napalm, but whatever it was, these planes provided good back-up in all three theatres.

Portuguese F-84 pilots stride out in front of the aircraft at Luanda. (José Tuna)

The F-84s provided exceptional close-air support for several years. As Cann tells us, they were deployed in Operation Onzo, launched to recover the settlement of Beira Baixa near the Congolese border with the pilots having to make precision drops of napalm canisters less than 300 metres from own forces because there were no 500-pound bombs or rockets available.

In covering the wars, I constantly spotted T-6 Harvards at forward airbases, both in the north and east of Angola (as well as in Mozambique and Portuguese Guinea, where they were a feature until the Italian G-91 jets arrived). The first four T-6s came as a gift from France—with markings removed—having been struck off the inventory and referred to rather flippantly as the 'F-110'. That was because it took off at 110 knots, and cruised and landed at that speed.

The Dornier Do-17 arrived soon after and became a regular feature of the war. The first time I was taken up in one was from Bissau's Bissalanca airport with João Bacar, an illustrious black *comandos Africanos* captain in charge of counterinsurgency measures in his sector. Not satisfied with going straight to his base at the heavily disputed Tite Barracks,* we spent ages over clumps of forest looking for an extremely elusive enemy. It didn't help that our Dornier wasn't armed. Normally that plane had an offensive capability of twin pods of eighteen 37mm rockets fitted to hard-points, one under each wing.

---

* Not to be confused with Tete, a city on the Lower Zambezi in Mozambique.

7. PORTUGAL'S COMMANDOS

"Portugal's commandos conducted numerous operations in the north of Angola, often using a combination of ground assault and helicopter envelopment. These more complicated operations generally yielded prisoners who provided valuable intelligence and caches of arms. In other instances commandos acted as part of a larger force in a coordinated effort and their function there was to serve as the hammer in a 'hammer and anvil' operation in which they drove the enemy into a waiting force and, hopefully, get caught in a crossfire."

John P. Cann, *Portuguese Commandos, Feared Insurgent Hunters, 1961—1974*

During one of my sojourns in eastern Angola, I was hosted by an enterprising young officer who headed the local *comandos Africanos* unit in what was then Vila Luso, today Luena. Captain Manuel Ferreira da Silva was still in his twenties when I first met him. I'd been told that he'd already been active in the war for quite a few years

Commanding Officer Carlos Fabião addresses the Regiment of Commandos. (Associação de Comandos)

and had a distinctive bunch of exploits both in Angola's east and north to prove it, plus an award or two for distinguished service, something he was not prepared to talk about.

His commando camp was basic and reflected few of the comforts of life that might be found in other military bases in Angola. Obviously, these men had a job to do and they got on with it. In any event, as I was discover, they were rarely in camp more than a few days at a stretch. Nor did I ask about numbers—their own, or those of the enemy. I was given a briefing and a map on the wall suggested that the teams operated in a vast region that stretched from Luso—on the main rail line into the Congo's Katanga—to the Zambian border, a distance of several hundred kilometres. It included the Cazombo Panhandle which had seen a lot of action since the initial days of Zambian involvement with the guerrillas.

Apart from ground deployments in Berliet as well as the Mercedes Unimog troop carriers, most *coup de main* actions were centred on helicopter target envelopment, referred to in the Portuguese language as a *golpe de mão*. There was a fairly large motor pool at the base, but it was made clear that a fair amount of movement was by Alouette helicopters (which doubled in ground support roles), with Aerospatiale Pumas only arriving fairly late in the war.

An Alouette hovers during an operation.

A Portuguese army unit takes a break in the bush during follow-up operations.

Though the Luso commando unit was similar in most respects to the all-African *comandos Africanos* (with whom I went to war in Portuguese Guinea a few years later) and shared the same motto—*Audaces Fortuna Juvat* (Luck Protects the Bold)—Captain da Silva's group was made up mainly of white troops from the *metrópole*, though there were also quite a few black Africans on the base.[*]

When first formed, the commandos, who could be identified by the distinctive bush knives they sported on their left shoulders, were organized into independent/intervention units or groups composed of volunteers from infantry battalions. Success in the field followed fairly quickly, which meant that they were soon to be tasked to conduct special operations, usually under direct orders of the Angolan commander-in-chief.

The group's organization, for example, was one command team (an officer, signaller, medic as well as two soldiers), three 'manoeuvre teams' (one NCO and four soldiers) and a back-up team (an NCO and a RPG-armed troop, an 'ammunition' soldier as well as a couple more troops). This organization—a group with five teams and each team with five men—went through several adaptations, but the base cell—the fundamental five-men team—remained entrenched for the duration of Portugal's African wars.

---

[*] Al J. Venter, 'Report on Portugal's War in Guiné-Bissau'.

Commandos debus from their Unimog troop carrier during an ambush. (Associação de Comandos)

Fairly early on, the evolution of hostilities revealed the necessity of more commando soldiers—independent units capable of operating for longer operational periods in remote, difficult regions and completely self-sustained. That initially led to the creation of the commando element: its first company was formed in Angola. The history of the Portuguese commandos began on 15 June 1962 at Zemba, northern Angola, when the first six groups of Special Forces troops known as the Hunter Battalion, their predecessors, was formed. For preparation, the CI 21—*Centro de Instrução de Contraguerrilha* (Counter-Guerrilla Instruction Centre)—came into being commanded by Lieutenant-Colonel Nave. He had as one of his instructors the photographer and former French Foreign Legion sergeant Dante Vacchi, a legendary Italian national who had seen action in the Indochina and Algerian wars.

The six groups that emerged achieved excellent operational results. Nonetheless, Angola's command structure decided to re-evaluate the instruction and integration of these units into the army and early 1963 created the first of two principal instruction centres (CI 16 and CI 25) at Quibala in Angola.

For the first time, the term *commandos* was applied to the soldiers who qualified there. Jack Cann makes the interesting observation in his book on the Portuguese commandos that some years before the Angolan troubles, somebody in Lisbon was perspicuous enough to sense that with things rapidly changing in Africa, there might come a time when military force might be required to keep things in check, not only in Angola but also in Mozambique and Portuguese Guinea. Consequently, in June 1958, the minister of the army ordered Major Hermes de Araújo Oliveira to France to study French perspectives on counterinsurgency with the purpose of using this knowledge for training. Oliveira spent ten days in Paris and a month in Algeria talking to many key French officers involved in a war which had become bitter and destructive. On his return to Portugal, he started to prepare the groundwork that would create army units with the capability of fighting using these new techniques. His work extended to the creation of such units, and thoughts garnered in France were extensively described in his book *Guerra Revolucionária* [*Revolutionary War*].* This work explained the nature and organizational principles of the Portuguese commandos, inspired largely by what Oliveira had observed while with the French Foreign Legion and latterly with the Belgian Para-Commandos. The emphasis, he stressed throughout, lay in flexible mobility and creativity as well as in counter-guerrilla combat techniques.

As the Rhodesian war developed some of the tactics used by that country's Fire Force was adapted to Portuguese conditions in Africa, and vice versa. Eventually, the South African air force also played a role, some of its pilots detached to serve with Portuguese units fighting in southern Angola. Cann continues:

As the project developed momentum, a commission was formed of majors Oliveira, José Alberty Correia, José Pinto Soares, and José Henriques da Silva to explore the creation of what was termed Small Units for Immediate Utilization.

This commission produced two reports and detailed the creation and organization of 'Shock Units.' Later these were renamed 'Assault Troops' and designated '*caçadores*' from which stemmed the 'Hunter' unit concept.

In April 1959 (two years before the Angolan war started) the project entered a new phase, and the army authorized the establishment of its Centre of Instruction for Assault Troops (*Centro de Instrução das Tropas de Assalto* or CITA) at Lamego in Portugal's north. It set as a goal the establishment of a battalion of four companies that together would form the Battalion of *Caçadores* 5 (BCaç 5). These companies of Special Hunters (*companhias de caçadores especiais* or CCEs) would be formed from the CITA classes which would be filled with volunteers from serving troops.

In July 1960, CITA was recast as the Centre of Instruction for Special Operations (*Centro de Instrução de Operações Especiais* or CIOE) with twenty-one officers, thirty-five sergeants, and 319 men assigned. Graduates of the CIOE would carry the designation *caçadores especiais* and would have received what was termed special instruction in operational readiness (*instrução de aperfeiçoamento operacional*).

---

* Hermes de Araújo Oliveira, *Guerra Revolucionária*.

For those developing the curriculum and training for this 'operational readiness instruction' and the new reality of counterinsurgency, it became evident that a modification of old methods would not work. It was already accepted that this effort was going to be as much a psychological war as a physical one. Hence entirely new units had to be created, and their training tailored to confronting this new adversary. Instruction emphasized the techniques of combat as well as the psychological preparation for battle.

The psychological component was perhaps the most important and distinctive to the training, as its objective was to transform the recruit into a disciplined, competent, and confident soldier who would be able to adjust to all circumstances and fight effectively. The training was marked by a high degree of realism and the endless execution of procedural drills to make fighting second nature to the soldier. By September 1959, the initial three companies of the battalion had been formed and by April 1960 the men graduated.

The final and fourth CCE followed two months later in June, and all four were deployed to Angola that month. They wore the new brown beret and the first camouflage uniforms ever issued by the Portuguese army. It now appeared that Portugal was changing its army to fit the demands of an approaching war rather than trying to change the war to fit its army. These new troops were trained for and adapted to the environment in which they were expected to fight. While these measures were regarded as an important first step, 480 troops with advanced infantry training were not enough to make a difference in the crisis of northern Angola once hostilities had commenced.

As the war progressed, particularly the reoccupation of the north, the urgent need for additional specially trained troops became clear, that is those troops whose training would extend well beyond the traditional instruction and even beyond that of the CCEs. Such troops would be formed into units capable of operating independently for extended periods in the field.

Finally an insightful but still relatively young officer who was later to turn the war around in Angola, Lieutenant-Colonel Bettencourt Rodrigues was given a free hand in creating a new centre for training commandos. This would be at Zemba, a site about 150 kilometres northeast of Luanda, a first step and test model for expanding each Special Force unit. It was listed as the Battalion of *Caçadores* (*BCaç*).

Nine criteria were to evolve as to what was required of prospective commandos and these were detailed in orders: all new recruits had to be volunteers, with the ability to read and write. Each one of them had to be physically fit, agile and able to resist extreme fatigue. It was a *sine qua non* that they had to display extraordinary capacities of commitment as well as spirit of self-sacrifice. Finally, the

An Alouette gunship with the lethal 20mm Hispano cannon.

chosen few needed first-rate reflexes and were shown to be neither impulsive nor emotional.

Initial deployments were designed to accommodate groups of thirty men from each of the BCaçs operating in the north, and these would return as a 'commando group' to their assigned battalion and provide an example for others to follow. The project was theatre-specific in that it addressed the particular conditions in the north of Angola and taught its recruits how to fight the guerrillas in human and physical terms.

This aspect was regarded as pivotal. While the lessons from Algeria and Indochina were relevant—as taught by Oliveira and Vacchi—each insurgency was obviously very different and local adjustments to fighting insurgency successfully were critical. One of the skills introduced, Cann explains, was that of helicopter insertion into the battlefield:

> This was facilitated with the arrival of six new Alouette III helicopters from late 1962 and into the spring of 1963. With these, a section of four men, sometimes five could be inserted, and ultimately five Alouette IIIs were deployed to place a

combat group of twenty commandos on the ground. Later these were supported by a sixth helicopter that had a 20mm cannon mounted to the rear of the pilot.

The composition and organization of commando companies were always adapted to the specific circumstances and situations encountered, although throughout the war it was possible to verify two main models that originated what we can call light companies and heavy companies.

The former were composed of four commando groups, each one with four sub-groups, constituting eighty men and with few back-up components. These companies had little of the capability needed to maintain themselves independently during long periods of time, because their role was primarily as temporary reinforcements to units in *quadrillage*, as in 'intervention forces'.

So-called 'heavy companies' had five five-team commando groups, in a total of 125 men, together with a formation of service personnel (about eighty troops, with medics, signallers, transport soldiers and cooks). Another type of organization was adapted to the companies of African commandos, formed in Guinea.

Although Angola's Commando Instruction Centre was the unit HQ, it was there that the main core of commando doctrine evolved. That said, it was taken for granted that all battalions routinely gave instruction to their staff and formed units to intervene in the various operational theatres.

At the end of the day, commando units active in Africa constituted about a single percentage point of all forces active in these colonial wars. But their casualty rate was easily ten times higher than those incurred by regular forces. It was also accepted that these Special Forces units eliminated more guerrilla fighters and captured more weaponry than all the other units combined.

After the war, the commandos continued to develop their skills until 1993 when they were disbanded. This decision was influenced by a number of deaths during instruction. They were merged with the paratroopers and these were transferred from the air force to the army.

8. THE WAR IN THE EAST

While much of Angola's war was focused in the north, adjacent to the two Congos, the east and southeast soon came into play. This was a vast, underpopulated region, much of it rolling savannah and, indirectly, host to the evolvement of landmine warfare in Africa. It was the landmine, both anti-tank—which could blow away a ten-truck or a Unimog with a bunch of troops on the back—or the anti-personnel bomb—which caused the most damage in the minds of the soldiers who were fighting this war that ultimately altered the pace of Africa's liberation wars.

The reality of it was there for everybody to see: men lying on the ground beside their vehicles after the blast waiting for a helicopter to fly them to hospital. But that only happened if they were lucky, because most times in Lisbon's colonial conflicts there were simply not enough of these machines to call into action. Generally it was the unit medic who was called upon to do his thing, though front-line medics in the Portuguese army, however well trained, were hardly qualified to deal with amputations and major trauma.

In reality, the nature of the war was that the men involved could hardly miss the terrible injuries inflicted by these bombs which were customarily laid in a few centimetres of shallow dirt and needed only a few kilos of pressure to explode. The burns alone were horrific: the average Soviet TM-46—or its successor, the TM-57—generated something like 3,000°C heat and any exposed part of a soldier's body, an arm or a leg for instance, was instantly incinerated.

Yet, there were some unusual landmine 'survival' stories in both the Rhodesian and the Angolan wars. I met the driver of an army Bedford truck in Rhodesia's Operation Hurricane whose front wheel had detonated a mine. He survived almost without injury because the blast went directly between his extended legs without creating more than a few patches of superficial burns. As he explained, a sheet of flame erupted through the floorboards and blasted through the roof of the cab. That that happened to him twice in about a month.

More often than not, after a vehicle had detonated a mine, the convoy would come to a halt and if it was not under attack in an ambush, the men would gingerly step out, only too aware that if an anti-tank mine had been laid, there would probably be quite a few anti-personnel ones as well. As the saying went: it there's an anti-tank, there are bound to be APs. Most times the sappers would be called forward to clear the area before any kind of free movement was permitted. But all that took time. In the interim there was no thought given toward possibly looking for tracks and going

A trooper warily scans the jungle canopy.

after the rebels who had originally laid the charges. Attention would be focused on the immediate and by the time the convoy got moving again, it would quite often detonate another deadly device a few kilometres or so up the track. For this reason, the Portuguese moving about the east would ignore existing vehicle tracks and would make their own roads in the sandy wastes of a region that previous generations had long ago dubbed *terras fim do mondo*: lands at the end of the earth. I would fly over some of it and would sometimes see a dozen different sets of tracks leading in roughly the same direction, each one studiously avoiding the other because of mines.

To fully understand how Portugal fought its African wars, one needs to look closely at how individual units operated, sometimes fully integrated into fairly large 'families' under the control of one man, their commander. He was there to greet them when they arrived for training at army reception bases in Europe and it was he too that saw them through their entire deployment. He travelled by ship with them to Africa and then spent the next two or three years husbanding their affairs and, when it was over, he'd come back home with them. It was also his job to communicate with the parents of those who became casualties.

One such a man was Captain Vitor Alves. I spent ten days with this illustrious officer and his unit at N'Requinha, arguably the most distant camp in the entire Angola.

It was a place where even the Atlantic seemed remote. As the crow flies, this isolated military base—almost within sight of the Zambian frontier—was actually closer to Mozambique on the Indian Ocean than to the Angolan capital. Few Portuguese army officers I encountered during the course of several visits to Lisbon's three African possessions at war at the time were quite as dedicated to what they were doing as this unassuming, yet astonishingly perspicacious young man who was rarely fazed by the problems he faced. He made no secret of the fact that though he was married to Teresa, the daughter of an admiral, he was a socialist and believed implicitly that his was a war that could not be won by force of arms. Still, he was a good soldier and did what his superiors expected of him.

In a sense, Captain Vitor Alves was guardian, mentor, confident and protector to everybody within his fief, including hundreds of African refugees who returned to Angola after having been shanghaied to Zambia by the rebels. It was these pathetic souls who, desperate to get back to their original bush villages, had escaped their captors—sometimes with their entire extended families—and landed on the captain's N'Requinha doorstep.

On average, Alves' troops fought perhaps one action a week. Some might be half-hearted contacts where few shots were exchanged; others were more intense, usually

A patrol in eastern Angola, a tedious process with mine detectors.

Casevac!

as a result of being ambushed. At the same time, there was nothing reminiscent of the intensity of what was going on just then in Vietnam because it was not that kind of war. At other times, vehicles heading in his direction with supplies might be ambushed, which was when things tended to get serious

Under his command, Captain Alves had a company of 165 men and five officers and in spite of distances—and an obvious lack of manpower, as well as inadequate firepower because he had no artillery—he seemed to manage. While most actions since the unit had arrived at N'Requinha eight months before had been fairly low key—Alves had lost one man with three wounded, one seriously—the unit's tally of guerrillas killed, wounded and captured was impressive. It numbered scores but, he conceded, that trend also demonstrated shortcomings in insurgent basic training, discipline and lack of commitment.

To reach the captain's base, I had to travel eastward by air from Luanda in a Nord Noratlas and pass through the diamond centre of Henrique de Carvalho (Saurimo today).

We touched down for lunch at the Luso rail junction near the Congolese frontier with the last leg in a German-supplied Unimog. In the process we covered more than 2,000 kilometres.

The camp at N'Requinha was astonishingly self-sufficient. It grew its own vegetables and the captain had a modest herd of cattle, pigs and goats, all of which helped supplement the community's diet, isolated as it was from the rest of the country. Most supplies arrived by road and the columns often only reached them once a month, having usually detonated the requisite number of mines along the way.

An interesting group at N'Requinha were the Bushmen. These tiny San people had lived for thousands of years in the Kalahari Desert, farther south, but were also found in many parts of southern Angola. Their community at the base numbered about twenty.

"They've suffered badly ... the enemy ... they're often hunted like wild dogs. I hire them for what they've always been best at ... trackers and hunters ... and their traditional enemies pay the price," said Alves.

Although these remnants of a Stone Age culture had assimilated a few Western customs—they liked their liquor and the white man's tobacco—they had lost none of their age-old talents for tracking. In those distant, sandy wastes, they could pick up trails, that to my eyes were completely invisible and they'd tell me that they were three or four days old.

"My Bushmen here can smell the presence of humans, sometimes from a kilometre away. Then they would go on and tell me whether they're black or white ... quite remarkable when you think about it," the captain said. If there were any whites in the enemy column, the Bushmen were immediately animated about the prospect of a contact. Europeans—Cubans, Russians or journalists—with the guerrillas was a bonus in their eyes and they viewed their task as one to hunt him down. Basil Davidson, the British writer who accompanied several guerrilla combat groups into Angola and wrote a book about his experiences in the African bush had at least one close shave after being tracked by Bushmen. One enemy unit that Davidson accompanied laid dozens of landmines.

There was no question that these little people were outstanding operators under the bizarre and primitive conditions in what verged on a desert-type environment. More than once they had flushed insurgents out of a thicket, Portuguese army *Alferes* (or 2Lt) Manuel 'Zapata' Martins admitted, adding that he had two Bushmen in his group and he had been out on many long-winded slogs into the sparse bush country with them. He called them "the little people" because most were barely five feet tall and they always marched right alongside him while on patrol but moved to point when onto something they considered 'hot'. 'Zapata' was twenty-two years old, a professional soldier who had been in the army for four years. Of Jewish extraction, his parents had arrived in Portugal from Spain during the Civil War.

A group of guerrillas, in fine fettle—well fed, clothed and armed.

At Serpa Pinto, farther west, I was later to meet the famed Bushman anti-terrorist leader 'Satan', who was reputed to have killed more of the enemy than any other black man in Angola. 'Satan' was a deadly shot with his favourite rifle, another old KAR-98. Reputedly, he could pick off the enemy at 500 metres, *without* the advantage of telescopic sights. This grey-haired old man was surprisingly agile for his years. He earned his name as a result of the ritual to which he subjected all his victims. As soon as he'd killed a man, he would slit open the chest and cut out the man's heart. Only then would he be satisfied that he had sent him "to join his forefathers". 'Satan' smiled approvingly while his story was related with the help of an interpreter, another Bushman, both men totally oblivious of the fact that the Geneva Convention might oppose such actions.

The Portuguese were certainly not about to change his habits because the man was extremely good at his job.

Captain Alves explained that the war in his area differed markedly from similar campaigns being fought in the Luso region well toward the north. The fighting was more tenuous and over a wider front, he explained, since the enemy were not intent on making contact with Portuguese units so close to the frontier where he was based. Their orders were specific: infiltrate through Sector CC to the west and join their comrades in taking the war to the hated colonials.

"They come through here from staging areas in Zambia, most times well-armed and stocked, many of them struggling with heavy loads intended for the distant interior." He reckoned the situation might almost be equated to Sector D north of Luanda, though without the jungle.

"This hinterland is far more exposed and they have to get all the way across, sometimes in large groups because their support crews accompanied them and sometimes their women. It is our job to stop them," he added.

When contact was made with an insurgent group, he explained, it was not simply a matter of trailing them through the bush and trying to force them to make a stand. "Retaliatory stands were a given, so were ambushes. Yet, if terrain allowed, our forces would try to leapfrog ahead and set up ambushes." Ideally, he said, he'd liked to have a couple of helicopters on hand to be able to move his men around.

Alves had tried a number of tactics in the time he and his men had been at this isolated base, a few of which had been reasonably successful. In his first few months at the base he and quite a large squad of his men had trailed a group for more two or three weeks and were eventually responsible for the death or capture of an entire MPLA infiltration group.

"That was my symbolic forty days of isolation in this wasteland ... tough, often disheartening and in the end, quite nasty. But it was stamina and perseverance that did it for us ... in conjunction with two units that were brought in as things started to develop and we ended up killing thirty one and capturing a dozen."

A mine-clearing operation about to start.

Patrols had to maintain a wary eye for AP mines.

It was on that operation that the he had lost a man, while a sergeant had been badly wounded in the leg and gut. The captain maintained that black soldiers in the Portuguese army were capable of surviving far more serious wounds than most Europeans, certainly far better than his own troops. In a training exercise in the Dembos, shortly before his unit had been posted to N'Requinha, one of his African corporals had been wounded. He'd been shot by a large-calibre rifle, or what hunters like to call an elephant gun. The blast had done terrible damage to his ribcage but, quite remarkably, the bullet had not penetrated any of his vital organs. "His entire chest was cleaved open ... obviously we were left with a shocking mess to deal with and our medical orderly was ill while treating that poor fellow. When we got him back to base the priest offered Last Sacraments before he was taken out by helicopter. The man survived, and while it has taken time, he'll be back with us in a month or two."

The captain stressed that this remarkable natural resilience was one of the reasons why the insurgents had been so successful: "They can take much more punishment than we can."

Alves had just returned from a long chase through southeastern Angola a few days before I arrived at N'Requinha. He had been tasked by radio to help 'Zapata' follow a band of infiltrators, zigzagging for something like a hundred kilometres through the bush along the Zambian frontier:

> We were out for weeks and in our chase the enemy would try an occasional half-hearted ambush and then rush off again, obviously eager to shake us off rather than doing anything confrontational. In fact, they'd never allowed us any kind of meaningful contact. So I tried something that had worked once before, with my predecessor who had thoroughly briefed me while we were still in the north.
>
> Altogether, there were about eighty men in the patrol, which, for us, was a lot, but then some enemy units could be 300-strong and we needed strength in numbers which made for an additional nightmare in keeping them supplied. So when we reached a large abandoned *quimbo* [native village] on the Luiana River, I split my group, picked eighteen of my best men and sent the rest back to base ... I kind of made it look like we'd all gone home.
>
> We spent the first night hiding in the deserted village and though the routine established was that half the men stood guard while the others slept, I doubt whether anybody got any real shut-eye: there was always something on the move in the bush like hyenas or other predators.

Another landmine victim.

It was another day and a half before the enemy showed up, but then disappeared again for no apparent reason, Captain Alves explained. He was prepared to wait three days and his patience was rewarded because the main body of the insurgents appeared on the third evening.

It was a tough call, far more so than any other place I've waited in ambush. We were all aware that they were somewhere in the vicinity, which meant that we couldn't speak among ourselves or even smoke … everything was tense. A single spot of light in the dark would have revealed everything.

Suddenly there was a bunch of them approaching the village. Across from the *quimbo* there was a clearing about 200 metres away. They waited and watched for about twenty minutes before they decided that things looked OK. They stopped a second time about a hundred metres from where we were and by now we were more than ready for them.

I could see that all was not well during their second halt. They were in the middle of the clearing but someone at the head of the pack sensed that something wasn't quite right and that made them all uneasy. But they were well spread out, armed, with a handful whispering to each other, probably weighing up the odds.

That was when I decided that the best action would be to take them on immediately … I was worried that they'd withdraw. The best shot in the company was alongside me, my NCO sharpshooter. The arrangement was that if the rebels did stop some distance from the camp, he'd try to pick off as many as he could if I told him to go for it. That would also be the signal for the others to engage … and that is exactly what happened.

The sergeant killed three men with his first three shots even before they knew what was happening. By this time everyone was firing and the chase was on.

Captain Alves said the action lasted only a minute or two during which time a dozen guerrillas were killed within a short distance from where the first shots were fired. Among the dead they later identified a well-known MPLA group leader who called himself 'General' Kulunga.

9. CABINDA: TINY ENCLAVE ACROSS THE CONGO

"One of the most significant aspects of guerrilla warfare is the manifest difference between information available to the guerrilla and that available to the enemy."

Che Guevara, on his return to Cuba after visiting the
Cabinda Front while in Congo-Brazza

First impressions of Cabinda start even before you reach the modest airport that serves the tiny Angolan enclave to the north of where the great Congo river flows into the Atlantic.

Smaller than Puerto Rico, Cabinda was originally created by the fusion of three historic African kingdoms, the Kakongo, N'Goyo and the Loango. Undeterred by historical precedent, Lisbon claimed it in the 1870s while the rest of Europe scrambled for their chunks of African real estate.

It was a fortuitous move. Though Cabinda boasts less than a million inhabitants— about the same as a century ago—some of the largest offshore oil reserves on the planet lie off its heavily foliaged shores, just thirty minutes' flying time from Luanda.

Cabinda has never been kind to the few Europeans who settled there. The region is covered by some of the most expansive tropical jungle to be found on any continent and apart from the guerrilla war which kicked off shortly after the UPA invaded northern Angola from the Congo, this is a region of malaria, yellow fever, dengue, skin parasites and a host of other tropical ailments that can kill a human in a day. Oil apart, this is not a friendly corner of the globe. It is interesting that Che Guevara thought so too when he visited the place in 1964, and might be one of the reasons why he decided to devote his efforts to South and Central America rather than Africa. Not that he did not try; he spent many months in remote parts adjacent to both the Congo and Angola and his diaries suggest that he did not get on all that well with some of the leaders who he regarded as egotistical.

Going to Cabinda during the course of covering the Angolan war was originally not on my agenda. Undeterred by a plethora of negative reports, I decided that having got that far, I'd cover the enclave as well, having already spent time in both the Dembos and eastern Angola. First impressions of the enclave were disappointing. Cabinda town was overrun by Americans and Europeans more intent on oil than hostilities in the adjacent jungle, so I did not linger. Picked up by two enterprising young army officers—Victor

A patrol in Cabinda takes a break.

Marques, our official interpreter, and twenty-one-year-old Tony Martins, already a veteran of the war—we headed unescorted out of town in an army jeep.

Both men had been in Cabinda almost two years and were due for discharge; clearly, they enjoyed the unexpected interlude. Looking after us was a change from an otherwise dreary and uneventful existence forced on most of the troops after the insurgents had been driven north years before. There was still the occasional ambush but the local rebels who were known by the acronym FLEC—Front for the Liberation of Cabinda—lacked both the kind of intent and vigour displayed by the insurgent armies fighting farther south.

"We'll travel by jeep, driving during the day and staying over at various army camps along the way," Tony told me. He suggested that there was little likelihood of any kind of action. "That's long past," he declared and we took his word for it. Consequently we travelled the first 150 kilometres through some really tough jungle country with only two G3 carbines and a clutch of grenades between us. The road leading north out of Cabinda town was better than I had expected. It was surfaced as far as Landana, a seaside village that had been a popular weekend holiday spot before the war for many of the Americans working there. After that, it led inland to the forests of the interior and the Congolese frontier.

The area along the coast between Cabinda and Landana was oil country in the traditional American sense. The bustling, gum-chewing, cussing influence was everywhere: every few kilometres or so, we'd discover huge oil drills standing almost phallus-like, naked and erect in the bush, looking totally incongruous alongside tall palms and mahogany giants. There was an atmosphere of industry about this untamed land and the Yanks were playing it to significant advantage, as they had elsewhere in Africa and the Middle East. In some places the oilmen had established caravan camps. These were temporary 'homes from home' which they had shipped in from the States for themselves and the occasional wife who was brave and perhaps foolish enough to take the risk, not of the war but of tropical disabilities. Some of these camps were surrounded by three-metre barbed-wire fences topped with spotlights and I imagined that on the periphery of every camp somewhere, there were electronic alarms that would get security guards running if ever attacked.

Tony said that all these precautions were typical American, and actually not for their own protection at all, but rather, intended to keep the Portuguese— whom they regarded as largely bucolic—*out*. The same applied to recalcitrant Africans, he suggested. Tony Martins was never shy to reciprocate some of the

A Unimog patrol in Cabinda, ideal ambush country.

anti-Portuguese sentiments he'd encountered among a few of the oil workers, but generally, he found them an amiable lot.

In all, there were about 500 Americans working in Cabinda at the time. Had there been no war, it would have been many times that. There were a lot more based on the offshore rigs that characterized this stretch of the West African coast as far north as Nigeria, together with another thousand or so expatriates in Cabinda town itself, under contract and again, mainly security people. Gulf Oil had been drilling in that region for a dozen years before they finally found oil in commercially exploitable quantities; when they eventually did, it was a bonanza. Although they were obliged to suspend operations during the worst of the terrorist raids in 1961, the machine gun and bazooka muzzles were barely cold before they moved in again.

Along the road to the north we passed much evidence of battles that had so viciously blighted the region after the 1961 invasion. Every thirty-five kilometres or so the derelict remains of a Portuguese army camp would loom out of the jungle. In most cases, their gates had long ago fallen off their hinges, their observation turrets and guard posts collapsed but nobody had bothered to remove the miles of barbed wire that surrounded every one of them. Some were almost surrealistically covered in creepers and lianas, like out of *Apocalpyse Now*.

The two officers formed an interesting contrast. Marques was an arts scholar who had spent several years at Coimbra University, his bearing and polished mannerisms

Troops deplane into thick elephant grass.

reflecting that of a well-placed family in the Metropolis. Like the rest, he had been conscripted to spend a couple of years in Africa and he loathed it. Obviously the Cabinda posting had not made life any easier and, as he admitted after his second glass of unchilled *vinho branco*, he had a somewhat unique take on his predicament: "If I'm going to be stuck in Africa for ten percent of my lifespan, then surely I'd have preferred to be where the action is," he commented. "Then there would have been interesting things to talk about ... and a risk or two, yeah!"

Tony Martins was a very different individual because he seemed to relish the uncertainty of war. Born in Angola, near the South West African border and close to a South African farming community—which was where he had been taught his English—he pulled out a photograph of his aged grandmother. It surprised me that she was black: "pure, authentic African," was the way he described her. He was very close to her, he said fondly, "a warm, really lovely soul". Among the words he used to describe her was something affectionately Portuguese that I cannot recall.

Grandma had married one of the early Portuguese traders and it was no surprise that Martins was enormously proud of his mulatto origins, though he could easily, as some would comment, have "passed for white" had he chosen to do so. He also admitted to being quite passionate about Africa generally and would call it "my oyster", adding that he had peered only briefly under its shell. The exploration he dreamed of and often talked about was still to come ...

Curiously, quite a few years later, after Lisbon had capitulated, I was to bump into Tony—by now a civilian—among a large group of refugees gathered together on the outskirts of Sa de Bandeira, later renamed Lubango. Not at all despondent—though clearly the future looked bleak because he and his family had lost everything—the former lieutenant was heading toward South Africa where he hoped to be able to make a new life for them all.

In Cabinda, just then, he admitted the area we were passing through was actually not as peaceful as some would have liked to make it. He confided that he often led his patrol for days along the Congolese frontier in search of insurgent groups and he'd find them too, even if he inadvertently strayed into what he liked to call "enemy territory". He never went so far as to admit to having set foot in either Kinshasa's Congo or Brazzaville's but then he'd chuckle quietly and change the subject or grab another Cuca beer from the cooler on the jeep.

Only when I got to know him better in the days ahead did he admit that he'd chased a group of insurgents—about fifteen-strong— across one of those unmarked frontiers. The guerrilla group believed they were safe and had stopped running, but not secure from the wiles of a cock-a-hoop Portuguese army lieutenant by the name of Tony Martins. He and his men killed half of them before the original infiltrators were even aware what was happening. The rest of the group was brought back to Cabinda

Early days in the Cabinda enclave when mine casualties took a toll.

in shackles. It caused a rumpus at the time and both he and his commanding officer were blasted by Luanda. The lieutenant ended up in the guard house for a while, though nothing ever appeared on his record, nor did he lose rank. The furore was eventually taken all the way to New York and Lisbon's representative at the General Assembly was obliged to admit that it had all been a terrible mistake: "Anyone would have thought I'd started the Third World War," Tony laughed when he got to the punchline. "And yes, it was a huge incident," adding that next time it happened, he wouldn't be bringing back any prisoners.

The following month, not altogether unexpectedly, he was decorated for bravery in a similar kind of action. Again, he'd sneaked across the border, linked up with some locals who were being persecuted by a bunch of *terroristas* and pinpointed an enemy camp. With his squad, many of them who had been with him in the first attack, he promptly set about ambushing one of their patrols. During the course of a firefight that lasted about ten minutes, he deliberately drew enemy fire while some of his men crept around and caught the insurgents in a crossfire.

"You see, you never know what those idiots in Luanda want. The one minute they jail me, the next they give me a medal," he exclaimed, gesticulating as he spoke.

Shortly after we'd passed though Landana we arrived at Cabinda's infamous 'Bridge of War'. There had been some serious fighting in the area early in 1961 and it marked one of the stages of the long trek south by some of the refugees, mostly African. Apart from the original battle which gave the place its name, its main claim to fame was that the bridge was never ever captured by the enemy. But afraid of the Portuguese, the refugees,

Fuzileiros prepare for action.

great numbers of them fearful of being shot by government troops, did not use the bridge either. They had to go some distance upstream and use boats, pirogues or barges, often clandestinely, to avoid patrols. Straddling a narrow, swampy outlet to the sea, the structure looked typical of many Bailey bridges erected by British army engineers in World War II, only this one had been built by Portuguese sappers after the insurgents had partly destroyed the original structure in 1963. By the time we got there, it was being guarded at both ends by a detachment of black and white soldiers: they took our names, passport details and the plate number on our jeep as we passed.

"From here on," said Lieutenant Martins seriously, "we don't know what lies ahead. That's why they take our details, which are passed on by radio to the next camp up the line. If we don't arrive, they come looking for us, or what's left of us," he joked.

The man had a wicked sense of humour. We halted on the far side of the bridge while Tony briefed us on the historic battle. By all accounts, the Portuguese army fought for almost a full day in the area around the bridge, one of the rare occasions that the guerrillas were prepared to match blow for blow in a stand-up fight.

"Across the border in the two Congos they still talk about the 'army that disappeared' and even today they don't know the true story." The jungle jealously guarded its secrets, was the phrase he used. "The battle started at dawn. There were about 300 troops on either side, facing off across this channel. The bridge was in the middle, or what was left of it after it had been mined." Earlier, the army tried a dangerous tactic. "Before dawn, and in total darkness, a small squad of our commandos moved around the edge of the swamp in rubber boats and were dropped off every couple of dozen metres or so. It wasn't long before our troops were positioned all the way around the morass. The idea was to make it look like they had surrounded the rebels," he explained

In theory the Portuguese *had* surrounded the enemy, but with only a few dozen men. It was a dodgy ruse because if those troops were cut off from their main body they might easily have been overrun.

"Then finally, when the onslaught was launched, just as it started to become light, it sounded like an entire Portuguese battalion had arrived … they fired guns, hurled grenades and even launched some mortar shells. The enemy held on for a few hours, but they hadn't been prepared for this kind of concerted action and eventually their efforts wavered, probably because they were running short of ammo."

It was late afternoon before the main group broke and ran. They had nowhere to go but into the swamp. "Our boys emerged from their positions and mowed them down … just like that … the handful that got away either drowned or they were taken by crocs. We didn't even have to bury their bodies."

The lieutenant estimated that Portuguese casualties numbered about six or eight, all killed in the first hour of the battle when the other side was still carefully directing its fire. He had since studied details of the onslaught and doubted whether the rebels would make the same mistake twice, not that they had much chance of that, he added.

In his two years in Africa, Martins had personally killed or captured twenty-three of the enemy, a figure he was initially reluctant to reveal. We eventually prised it out

Fuzileiros muck in to clear an obstacle in Cabinda. (Revista Militar)

of him on the fourth night at a mess dinner that ended with a recorded concert by Amalia Rodrigues. Even in darkest Africa, Fado ruled. The lieutenant's tally of kills was confirmed afterwards by Major Mathias, who noted that about half—double figures—were accounted for during sorties into Congo-Brazza.

Though not exactly a fan of the former Cuban guerrilla Ernesto 'Che' Guevara, Lieutenant Tony Martins—for reasons of his own—held the man in great respect. "He and I would have been on opposing sides had we met, but that doesn't prevent me from admiring the way he went about fomenting revolution. Before he was killed he was one of the greats in unconventional warfare ... we studied the same kind of tactics ... probably had a similar mindset when it came to inflicting damage."

Guevara, he was aware, had visited both Congos during 1964 and even spent a while at Dolisie, an insurgent training camp about forty kilometres north of the Cabinda frontier. That meant, Martins believed, that more likely than not, he'd entered the territory on a reconnaissance sortie, probably not far from where he was stationed at the time. Che was that sort of operative, Martins believed, and would not have passed up the opportunity.

"He probably even got a few Portuguese soldiers in his sights, though he never actually went into battle in these parts though he did in the Congo, briefly." Dolisie, he explained, was a major MPLA base staffed largely by Cubans, so it all made sense.

Part of our journey to the north of the enclave passed through one of the great natural tropical jungles of the world, Cabinda's magnificent Maiombe forest. At the time, the Portuguese claimed that only sections of the Amazon were denser, as does the present Angolan government. "You get lost in there and you're a goner," Martins warned. Since World War II, a number of aircraft had gone down in the forest and some of those wrecks had still not been found. Maiombe starts about fifty kilometres north of the 'Bridge of War' and forms part of a jungle chain that stretches from the Congo Basin near Boma, through Cabinda and Congo-Brazza all the way to the Maiombe plateau in Gabon, a distance of almost a thousand kilometres. I had seen parts of it while visiting Albert Schweitzer's jungle hospital at Lambarene a year before he died in 1965. It had taken me two days of travelling rough on an open boat up the Ogówe river from Port Gentil at the coast and along the way I was told that the river cut through a section of Maiombe.* The jungle growth on both sides of the Ogówe was overwhelming, something I have never seen since. It was peculiar because the river is relatively short but in places because of the rainfall, as every bit as wide as the giant Congo and quite as awesome. Much of it, I gathered, had always been regarded as impenetrable to man. Apart from forest giants, the terrain was interspersed by mangrove swamps that seemed to stretch halfway across Africa, much it a solid, unyielding morass.

---

*   My visit to his hospital at Lambarene in Gabon, where I met the great man only months before he died, is detailed in the opening chapter of the book *African Stories*.

A Portuguese conscript poses with his MG 42 and an extremely long belt of bullets at an improvised fortification.

Dinge camp, our destination in northern Cabinda, was like most military establishments in Angola. The garrison was about 200-strong, but there was rarely more than half that complement in camp at any one time. Most troops spent their time patrolling the surrounding jungle as well as the Congo-Brazza frontier which was only about twenty kilometres away. But because of the forest, that was a two-day trudge and it meant overnighting in the jungle, something Portuguese troops from Europe never got used to.

Although the men had not seen action for a while, the commandant explained that it was necessary to maintain optimum security: "When the rebels arrived before—in 1961—they caught us off guard. We won't allow that to happen again," he said. His fears were based on regular reports of another imminent guerrilla invasion, which, by the end of the colonial war, never came.

Dinge was surrounded by several machine-gun turrets, manned only during daylight hours. In any event, jungle in the vicinity was far too dense for the unit to depend on searchlights after dark.

"There are too many bushes and trees growing near the edge of the camp ... we cut them back, but weeks later they are there again, which happens in the tropics ... So, if we are to depend solely on lights and gun turrets, the enemy would be able to crawl through the forest right up to the fence. They would be on top of us before we knew where they were." For that reason, he explained, a number of patrols—a couple of dozen soldiers at a time—were always in the outlying bush. That was his concept of an early warning system and it seemed to work reasonably well.

As I had observed at Zala, across the river in Sector D, the men would station themselves in a relatively cosy position in the jungle—usually just off one of the larger tracks—and wait for the enemy to arrive. It was reasonably secure because the bush was too thick for anybody to creep up from behind.

Also, he intimated, you had to be a little crazy to go crawling around in that jungle on your hands and knees: "It's far more effective the way we have it. Also, the enemy is familiar with our system. They're aware that if they want to attack, they have to pass through our outer perimeter first."

The men had almost no trouble with wild animals: "They smell and see us long before we are aware of their presence, which tells us that they steer clear of the most terrible animal of all ... man," he added unsmilingly.

It was dinner time when we arrived at Dinge and the sun set shortly afterward, disappearing quickly over the horizon, as it always does in the tropics. In the few minutes before it became dark in this part of tropical Africa, the horizon would often change colour four, perhaps five times. At this camp it was even more impressive; the surrounding rain forest and swamps seemed to create their own diffusing prism, all of which added a new dimension to a dying day. Even the soldiers would sometimes halt in their tracks at sunset. They had been there almost two years and they were always awed by this ever-changing spectacle.

Portuguese *caçadores* taking a break.

10. WHY THE WAR WENT THE WAY IT DID

Portugal was the first European nation to arrive in Africa and the last to leave. Was the Portuguese presence in Africa different from that of other European nations? In trying to explain why Portugal fought so hard for thirteen years to prevent its provinces in the *Ultramar* from being lost, one has to consider that with centuries of experience of the so-called 'Dark Continent', Lisbon probably understood Africa a lot better than the other European powers who arrived later in Africa. Further, the rebellion in Angola's north in 1961 was nothing new. There had been many uprisings, rebellions and revolutions in the past, some minor and quite a few that needed maximum effort, time and manpower to quash.

When explaining why Lisbon had reacted so strongly to the Angolan attacks in the early 1960s, Prime Minister Salazar said on numerous occasions that the provinces were, as he phrased it, "an extension of Portugal itself". As he declared, "all three

After the coup—General António de Spinola (centre) with Admiral Costa Gomes (right) with Vitor Alves behind.

territories are part of Greater Portugal," adding that he was not going to allow centuries of what he liked to call "historic civilizing tradition" to give way to radicals with guns.

The consensus in Lisbon at the time was that this sort of thing had happened before and that the problems would eventually pass. Those 'in the know' would remind the populace that some of the early rebellions in both Angola and Mozambique had been extensive and had cost many lives. But, they would aver, it had never been in vain because all had been put down, some quite brutally, particularly in regions adjacent to German South West Africa (before World War I).

It is interesting that there are many recorded instances of South Africans having been hired to fight as mercenaries in some of the earlier conflicts; according to French historian René Pélissier, dozens of times in the century before.

What is astonishing is that Portugal was able to rally the way it did when, for a time, all seemed lost. One needs to recall that Portuguese civilians took the brunt of rebel fury and were indiscriminately slaughtered as and where they were found, never mind the tens of thousands of local people who were massacred.

One needs to accept, too, that while the Portuguese were not battling the most sophisticated enemy on the planet, the guerrillas quickly evolved into a fairly effective fighting force and were kept well supplied with the same weapons then being

It was landmines that eventually weakened the resolve of Lisbon in its African wars.

used against the Americans and her allies in Vietnam. Also, guerrilla cadres from all three territories were being trained in their thousands in military establishments behind the Iron Curtain, China and Cuba as well as in a dozen African states that enjoyed Moscow's support.

Politics apart, there were other reasons that ultimately led to Portugal being forced out of Africa and there is no question that in the modern period—post-World War II—there have been few conflicts that have been 'won' outright. Most recent wars have ended up at the negotiating table and what should have been fairly clear victories resulted in the 'winner' having to yield, often quite substantially: the Korean war (still undecided), Israel after the Six-Day War (the Jewish state having to hand back all of the Sinai Peninsula), American efforts in Vietnam, the Iran-Iraq war (one of the bloodiest) and South Africa's so called Border war. In most cases both sides claimed victory.

The same situation held with the Lisbon's African 'provinces'. The Portuguese did not lose its wars in Angola, Mozambique and Portuguese Guinea, but then she did not win them either. Like several other conflicts, everything eventually centred on politics, in this case driven by a disaffected military establishment. The reality is that the people who challenged Lisbon's hegemony for their freedom in these overseas territories eventually got it. At the same time, just about anybody involved could—should they wish to do so—see the writing on the wall that conditions in Lisbon's African dominions simply could not go on indefinitely like they had. The country was being bled dry by a war that pitted one of Western Europe's smallest and poorest nations against the might of the Soviet Union. One also has to take into account that everything that happened took place at the height of the Cold War, no small issue in the 1960s and 1970s. With the so-called 'Carnation Revolution', everything changed and it happened overnight.

Those who were there will tell you that the entire nation breathed a cumulative sigh of relief on the morning of 25 April 1974 when the 'Young Officers' declared that the war was over. Simply put, the nation was tired of conflict; the people were war weary.

Once large numbers of young men had started to vote with their feet and head abroad to avoid the call-up, it was only a matter of time before somebody had to call it a day. The politicians would not (and probably could not) so a bunch of dissident army officers did it for them. It is interesting that something similar happened in the Rhodesian bush war, though obviously on a much smaller scale. Prime Minister Ian Smith confided that he had been made aware of his country's military shortcomings when it was reported that he was losing between a company and a battalion of men to emigration every month. These were the same people who had been doing the fighting. They simply moved on: like the young Portuguese who fled abroad, they felt they simply had to, for the sake of their families and their careers. In both countries—as

Lisbon employed every possible resource to combat the enemy, including mounted patrols.

subsequently with South Africa—the consensus was that there was essentially no future in losing unnecessary lives in a succession of bloody African wars.

Which raises the question: Was Portugal ready to do battle on three very different and remote (from Europe) fronts in Angola, Guiné-Bissau and Mozambique? Additionally, some of these countries had several different areas of operation: Angola battled terrorism in the north and the east: Mozambique in the northern and central regions and Portuguese Guinea was taking a hammering on all four sides if you include the offshore islands which were much favoured by the PAIGC as clandestine operating bases. The answer is a resounding no and there are several reasons. The first and most salient is that of all the wars in the post-World War II epoch, Portugal was arguably the most 'unready' nation to embark on a major conflict, never mind one that lasted more than a decade.

One also needs to take into account that the Portuguese had almost no experience or training for an insurgency-backed war even in *one* of the overseas provinces, never mind three. The last time Portuguese troops had fired shots in anger was in World War I, and that was also in Africa (against Imperial Germany when it invaded Angola from the south). That the Portuguese army was able to haul itself out of what was clearly a soporific haze and rally to a cause that had suddenly become an extremely urgent 'do or die' affair was commendable, though, in the eyes of most European observers, it was totally unexpected, especially since the French had recently been driven out of Algeria. If the powerful and seasoned French army could not do it, ran the argument, how would an impoverished Lisbon shape in its bid to counter similar odds?

Then, to the surprise of all it wasn't long before young Portuguese troops were giving as good as they got. In record time these troops from Europe recaptured many of the gains made by the revolutionaries in northern Angola and the army was back on the offensive.

The difficulties faced by Lisbon were almost insuperable, finances being a major part of it: Portugal had very little cash to spare and it stayed that way for decades. Compared to today—with instant communications and jet travel—Angola might actually have been somewhere on the other side of the globe. Troops did not fly to Africa like the Americans did to Vietnam: they went by ship. All that took time, which was one of the reasons why it took months for the first large contingents to arrive in Luanda from Lisbon to back up the war effort. More pertinent, the country had no proper armaments industry. But again, it did not take long to get things going,

Roads were often non-existent, and the guerrillas destroyed many bridges.

first by acquiring the rights for the local manufacture of the G3 rifle (and several other weapons), acquiring the kind of heavy vehicles needed in a modern war and, of course, the vital air components that was an intractable part of it all. Some of this stuff was in place, but almost all was part of Lisbon's commitment to NATO and the Americans; obviously it helped immeasurably in the earlier phases. Then things started to change: though helpful at first, Lisbon's NATO allies—with a few significant exceptions—started restricting some of those assets for deployment to Africa. For a start, Washington wanted its jet fighters out of the war.

John P. Cann phrases it well when he declares that the Portuguese army was incredibly brave. Its men, he tells us "had the ability to fight under conditions that would have been intolerable to other European troops ... They could go for days on a bag of dried beans, some chickpeas and possibly a piece of dried codfish—all to be soaked in any water that could be found." He adds that they were able to cover on foot and through elephant grass and thick jungle distances of hundreds of kilometres over a three-day patrol period. They quickly learned how to fight well, and did so successfully for thirteen years across three fronts in regions that were almost half the size of Western Europe and stretched much of the distance across the African continent. There are few countries that fared as well in any guerrilla conflict in the past two centuries. But in the end it just became too much for this tiny nation and the self-elected leaders decided to move on, not without good reason.

Which now raises the matter of what I personally think about the Portuguese soldiers and their commitments? My sentiments are based solely on having covered these conflicts quite extensively over many years, all three of them. If you had to suggest today that there is any country that would send its boys into a war for more than a dozen years, you'd be laughed out of the room. The sentiment then and now is that it is an impossible concept, not only in terms of money but also manpower, logistical limitations and of course, the ultimate test: morale. Truth is, the youth of yesterday was a very different proposition to today's youngsters, and that applies as much to Portugal as it does to the average American, Israeli or British youngster fresh from school. Forty years or more ago young people accepted challenges as part of life because they had to.

One example puts this into perspective. When the Israeli army invaded Hezbollah strongholds in 2006, conscripts were ordered to leave all their personal electronic gear behind: cell phones, iPods, laptops and the rest. Many did not, with the result that when they called their families and their girlfriends from their bunkers inside Lebanon, Hezbollah communications specialists were able to triangulate those positions and rain mortars down on their heads. Also, can you imagine your son or your neighbour's son being sent to Africa for two years' military service without once being allowed to come home and without phones or computer games?

One of the curious rail cars used to protect Luanda's communications.

In the 1960s and into the 1970s, when war raged in Africa, those who were called up tended to accept their lot: it was part of the 'deal' of sharing a great part of Africa. It was only at later stages that many of these youths waiting to be called up slipped across the border and sought refuge in other countries, usually with the blessings of their families. For many, faraway Africa was as alien to the average kid who has just left school in Vila Real, Lisbon or Castelo Branco as landing on the moon, but then the majority accepted it uncomplainingly because it was considered in the national interest.

The same could probably said for Lisbon's adversaries, the MPLA, FNLA and UNITA in Angola, FRELIMO in Mozambique and, possibly the most successful guerrilla army of the lot, Amilcar Cabral's PAIGC in Portuguese Guinea. There is no question that guerrilla forces varied between the three overseas provinces at war, as they did in Rhodesia and with the South Africans along their frontier of Angola. In fact, as these wars progressed, the guerrillas improved markedly and those who arrived later learned a lot from many of the earlier incursions. Obviously, a good

A military parade in Luanda.

deal depended on basics such as training and education and, as hostilities dragged on, the ability to be able to handle complex weapons systems efficiently. Quite a few insurgents were killed laying anti-vehicle landmines that had been hauled hundreds of kilometres across country because they did not observe the basics: they ignored the simple task of keeping the detonator clean, so that when it was screwed into place it did not jam and you had no need to force it into the appropriate groove. That said, the guerrillas were a remarkably resilient force. They could march for weeks across tropical Africa and survive quite comfortably off the land. Few European troops—apart from Special Forces units—could, or would do the same. Locals facing them came from the land and very successfully lived off it. Also, the guerrillas liked to keep almost all their needs close by: their food, their weapons, ammunition and small stocks of medical equipment. That helps when you are active and mobile. Modern armies in contrast need an enormous amount of logistical backup. And those same Africans proved to be inordinately tough and uncomplaining. When wounded, I have seen black troops (both guerrilla as well as those serving in the Portuguese army) with horrendous wounds that would have killed most white youngsters.

BIBLIOGRAPHY

Cann, John P., *Counterinsurgency in Africa: The Portuguese Way of War, 1961–1974*, Hailer Publishing, St Petersburg, FL 2005

_____, *Flight Plan Africa*: *Portuguese Airpower in Counterinsurgency, 1961–1974*, Helion & Co., Solihull 2015

_____, *Portuguese Commandos: Feared Insurgent Hunters, 1961-1974*, Helion & Co., Solihull 2016

Cocks, Chris, *Fireforce: One Man's War in the Rhodesian Light Infantry*, 30° South, Durban 2006

de Araújo Oliveira, Hermes, *Guerra Revolucionária* [*Revolutionary War*], privately printed, Lisbon 1960

Devlin, Larry, *Chief of Station, Congo*, Public Affairs, New York 2007

Marcum, John A., *The Angolan Revolution, Volume II: Exile Politics and Guerrilla Warfare (1962–1976)*: MIT Press, Cambridge, MA 1978

Teixeira, Bernardo, *The Fabric of Terror: Three Days in Angola*, Devin Adair, Old Greenwich, 1965

Venter, Al J. & Friends, *African Stories*, Protea Books, Pretoria 2013

_____, *War Stories*, Protea Books, Pretoria 2012

Venter, Al J., *Battle for Angola: The End of the Cold War in Africa c. 1975–1989*, Helion & Co., Solihull 2017

_____, *Portugal's Guerrilla Wars in Africa: Lisbon's Three Wars in Angola, Mozambique and Portuguese Guinea*, Helion & Co., Solihull 2015

_____, *War Dog: Fighting Other People's Wars*, Casemate, Philadelphia, PA & Oxford, UK 2006

Index

About the Author

Al J. Venter is a specialist military writer who has had over fifty books published. He started his career with *International Defence Review*, covering military developments in the Middle East and Africa. He has been writing on insurgencies across the globe for half a century, involved with Jane's Information Group for more than thirty years. He was a stringer for the BBC, NBC News, as well as London's *Daily Express* and *Sunday Express*. He branched into television work in the early 1980s, producing more than a hundred documentaries, including *Africa's Killing Fields*, on the Ugandan civil war, and *AIDS: The African Connection*, which was nominated for a Pink Magnolia Award. His last major book, *Portugal's Guerrilla Wars in Africa*, was nominated for New York's Arthur Goodzeit military history book award. Venter writes extensively for several Pen & Sword military history series including 'Cold War 1945–1991' and 'A History of Terror'.